To Dave, Gail
& May
Thanks for your part
in the story so far.!!

West MSL
Ncy Blin

Nigel Bloxham's

Crab House Café

Simple rustic recipes from Dorset's famous seafood restaurant

Acknowledgements

I am deeply grateful to my friends and colleagues listed below for kindly agreeing to either help with, or appear within, the Crab House Café book! Without you, it would have been a very dull and laborious process, I'm sure!

Firstly, I'd like to thank my young brigade at the Crab House Café, both the kitchen and front of house staff members, who I know at some point must have thought that this book was only a figment of my imagination and never destined to become a reality!

I'd like to say a special thank you to Adam Foster, our head chef for six years now, and my son Charlie, who has played such an integral part in our success. Thank you for all your time, patience and encouragement over the years.

At this point, it is apt for me to thank my long-suffering family, who endure all things fishy! Without you, I would not have been able to come this far. Your belief in me has been inspiring by itself.

I also owe much of this dream to my grandmother, since she was the first person to take me into a commercial kitchen, when I was but knee high to a grasshopper! She showed me and taught me about the fresh ingredients that came in from the garden, often grown by my grandfather.

A big thank you must go to our die-hard customers, who come to the Crab House Café rain or shine, and also to our local suppliers for their wealth of knowledge, their passion, and their commitment to our ethos.

I must also thank the oyster farmers, Dave and Kyle, for rearing their 'babies', the now famous 'Portland Pearl' and 'Portland Royal' oysters. It is their job that everyone seems to want when the sun is out, but that nobody wishes for when there's a January or February storm brewing!

I would like to thank RMC Books for their help and creative encouragement, as well as our main photographer Tim Green and the Dorset guys, Daniel Rushall and Lara Jane Thorpe.

I would also at this point like to thank Mark Hix, the great British chef, for the wonderful foreword he has provided.

And last but not least, the one who has put up with the most... my wife Tracy! Thank you x

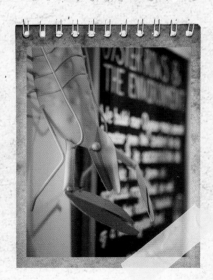

Foreword

We are blessed along the south west coast with great producers, and surprisingly to some, we have a fair few oyster fisheries on our doorsteps, including Nigel Bloxham's Portland oysters on the fleet. Portland oysters are the nearest oysters to our restaurant in Lyme, but we also offer them in our London restaurants, and if you know the Dorset coast you will have heard of Nigel's Crab House Café overlooking the oyster beds themselves on the fleet.

The Crab House Café is a little gem and serious about their fish and shellfish – well you would be I suppose, being responsible for the visible oyster beds in front of you which supply food shops and restaurants around the country.

Nigel has a knack for simply cooked seafood and adding interesting international twists to the dishes on the menu. A splash of local foraged seashore vegetables makes interesting eating – and reading.

Nigel and I often team up for local food festivals and talks on sustainability and fish in general. Food festivals are a lot of fun and sharing the knowledge that Nigel has with the locals and visitors is interesting, crucial and educational. You will be surprised how many people don't know about or how to eat what's abundant on our doorsteps.

Mark Hix

Welcome to the Crab House Café

It's commonplace in my quirky restaurant for customers to set about their food with hammers. I don't mind – in fact I positively encourage them to! It shows they're enjoying it. Other customers also do odd things from time to time – take the parrot who ordered chips! I found that a bit strange, considering that there were so many other tasty options on the menu!

It's not only the people who eat here that make the Crab House Café unique. We thrive on incorporating everyone and it's the colourful diversity of people that work with us that make the Crab House Café what it is today and why it's the passion of my life. From the spirited oyster farmer, to the baker who is also a Druid Priest, the passion runs through everyone and everything connected to the café... a passion for local produce and seafood. We are proud of our ethos that surrounds the need for naturally good food in a world where supermarket-sold, plastic-wrapped products are standard.

Diners from all over the world, who seek us out, often think they may have taken a wrong turn as they catch sight of the narrow, crumbling road from Wyke Regis that brings you to where the Crab House Café perches on the Jurassic Coast, along the Dorset seashore. Venture just a few metres further and they catch a glimpse of the restaurant, overlooking its own oyster beds and herb gardens, fronted by beaches where we gather sea beet.

We're known for many things, including the hammers as mentioned earlier and the wooden boards and bibs that we provide to customers about to sample our legendary freshly cooked crab.

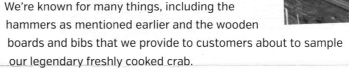

For the moment, however, I'd like to pause and reflect – it's that kind of day. As I write this at one of the Crab House's wooden dining tables, looking out towards wintry Chesil Beach, with the balloons and half finished drinks from last night's end of season party scattered around me, I can't help but reminisce about the journey that has led us to this point.

My interest in food, and particularly seafood, started in my early childhood. We always lived close to the water and from my home in Kingskerswell, South Devon, I would eagerly ride my bicycle to Torquay seafront to go fishing.

My grandfather was the gardener at the Charlton Park Estate and my grandmother the cook. They lived on the estate there and I have vivid memories of going to see them and being bowled over by the huge greenhouses. I can still recall the smell of the hot interiors, the sight of all the fresh food being grown, including grapevines, melons and asparagus. There were beautiful walled gardens, with a lake set amongst them. Part of my grandfather's job was to grow red roses so that the man of the house could have one every day – something that added to the romance of the place and created a lasting picture in my mind. However, it was there in the great kitchens of the estate, watching my grandmother cook, using all the wonderful, fresh produce, that the seeds were sown for my lifelong passion of cooking and producing wonderful dishes to be enjoyed by all.

When I turned 14, I was offered the choice between woodwork and domestic science at my all boys' school. For me, there really was no contest. So for those couple of hours a week, off to the girls' school I went! From there it was but a short step to training as a chef and my life's direction had been decided.

Today, the Crab House Café has its own team of dedicated chefs, whose enthusiasm is infectious! They are the special ingredients in our recipe for success. Visitors of various nations, as well as the national press, often make a beeline for the restaurant.

If I had to say why, it's perhaps because there's a certain yearning for the simple, what-you-see-is-what-you-get approach light years away from the ever-growing legion of chain restaurants with their standardised food that is the same wherever in the country you might be.

We're dedicated to serving what's good and what's local. We don't for instance – to the surprise of many diners – have king prawns on the menu. That might sound strange for a seafood restaurant, but for us it's a matter of principle. We only cook produce that we source directly from the locality at peak freshness. So you'll find only prawns that are caught in the Fleet just outside our window – for the few weeks they are available.

There's a certain yearning for the simple, what-you-see-is-what-you-get approach light years away from the ever-growing legion of chain restaurants with their standardised food that is the same wherever in the country you might be.

Eccentric? Maybe we are. But there's nothing better than the natural treasures that come from the sea off the Dorset coast.

We believe in championing the cause of seafood. As one of my acquaintances put it, once you get the scales under your nails, there's no going back. My career path was decided once and for all during a happy time I spent working for a fish supplier at Brixham Fish Market.

The boss said I was good with the restaurants and chefs, because as a trained chef myself, I knew what they wanted. So I spent my time packing, delivering and selling seafood and loving it.

When he announced he wanted to sell the business, I bought into it. The whole game got more competitive as time went on though and because of my skills as a chef I started to see other opportunities emerging. I watched as cuttlefish wasn't used and just lay on the quayside, rotting. I looked into it more and discovered how the Italians turned it into a delicacy by marinating it. I set up a company marinating cuttlefish and other seafood. We won our first national order and the business went from strength to strength.

The cuttlefish episode is one of many similar stories. It is sad but true that so many people seem so scared of seafood and unsure about how to handle it, prepare it and cook it. They seem to think that if they don't cook it properly it will poison them. This is a great shame and something I want to help change with this book.

The same applies in the restaurant. Often a customer might be a little uncertain about trying certain seafood. If they're completely new to the idea, we might start them with a meaty fish such as huss served with a red wine sauce and then move on from there.

Wherever possible we grow our own produce, including vegetables and herbs, and supplement this with plenty of foraging, for unsung ingredients such as sea beet and sea purslane. We even infuse our own spirits and oils using garden ingredients. This creates some wonderful discoveries, such as rhubarb and ginger vodka, sloe gin, rosemary and chilli oil to name but a few.

I am very lucky to have a young and dynamic kitchen team at the Crab House. Chef Adam Foster has been with us since 2007. He applies his talents to experimentation with new ideas, and as I write he's working hard on next season's menu. It should be an interesting one.

Everyone who works here is a highly-valued member of the team and I like to think they really are part of the Crab House Café family.

Everything is a joint effort and we like it that way. Our staff tends to stay with us – even if some occasionally go to pursue other opportunities, only to boomerang back – which we feel is testament to the family environment we nurture.

Everything is a joint effort and we like it that way. Our staff tends to stay with us – even if some occasionally go to pursue other opportunities, only to boomerang back – which we feel is testament to the family environment we nurture.

It's sometimes said that we're a bit Italian in the kitchen. But if we shout or wave our arms about, it's because we're passionate about what we do. And the customers seem to enjoy the show. One even left a separate tip to cover the entertainment.

Our son Charlie is a trained chef who has put in more than a few shifts in the kitchen. When we first took over the site he was only 14 and he used to come to work with me and go out on the boats. It gave him a strong appreciation of where the raw product comes from and also a massive respect for fishermen. He ran our front of house for three years, during which time we gained and maintained rosette level. He did a sterling job, but I think he would like to get back into the kitchen if he could. I know he enjoys contributing to all the discussions we have about new recipes and is always ready to comment.

And so to the baker with the unusual sideline. You could say he really makes his mark on the job, since his loaves are decorated with a geometric pattern, which it turns out is some kind of pagan symbol.

And the parrot? Yes, a customer did once bring his parrot along and its party piece was to request an order of chips. How could we not oblige?

There are more tales of life at the Crab House which we hope will give you a flavour of what we do. But for now, we'll do what we do best and let the food do the talking.

The Oysters

To those who have once sampled them, they are an incomparable delight, a pure and beguiling taste of the sea.

At the other end of the scale, there are the uninitiated, to whom eating an oyster is akin to skydiving or doing a bungee jump into a bottomless crevice. They're intrigued by the idea, but afraid to make the leap.

It's something we're well aware of, which is why we like to gently introduce sceptics to the idea.

I well recall a regular customer – he'd book a table for himself at the same time every week – who finally one day plucked up the courage to take the plunge.

We started him off with a cooked oyster. On his next visit he moved on to the raw variety. Realising what he had been missing, he was soon placing a regular order for half a dozen of the best as his starter course.

It seemed somehow appropriate, and gave us immense pleasure, when he found a pearl in one of his oysters some time later. Congratulations Mr Moule! And yes, that really was his name.

PLEASE DO NOT DIG
BETWEEN POSTS
OYSTER FARM TRACK WAY

Oysters feature large at the Crab House Café. That's hardly surprising given that we have our own oyster beds just a few yards away in the Fleet Lagoon.

There have been oysters growing in the Fleet since Roman times. We took over the site, which belongs to Lady Charlotte Townshend's estate, in 2005. It took two-and-a-half years of hard work to clear the old oyster beds. The project was not without incident. Disaster struck more than once when diggers became stuck fast in the Fleet.

But it was worth it.

The sea waters flood in twice a day, mixing with the fresh water which runs into the river from the chalky Dorset streams. This contributes to the oysters' sweet and slightly salty taste.

I believe we have the best oysters in the country. And it's not just me who thinks so. We won a 3 Star Gold Award for our Portland Pearl Oysters in the 2011 Great Taste Awards. We also won a 2 Star Gold Award for our Portland Pacific Oysters.

The Native Oyster (Ostrea edulis) has always been prized and was the oyster of choice until recently when disease, overfishing and pollution seriously depleted wild stocks. The more robust Pacific Oyster (Crassostrea gigas) has since taken its place in the marketplace and is the preferred oyster for cultivation worldwide. These are the oysters now grown in the Fleet.

To ensure the best results, we introduced a new and innovative oyster growing system called Aquapurse from Australia. It consists of timber posts and rows carrying purpose-made enclosed plastic baskets. The baskets rock with the ebb and flow of the tide and this rolls the oysters around as though they were on the sea bed. It helps create a smoother shell and fatter meat. It's rather like the difference between a battery-raised chicken and a traditional free-range one.

Part-grown oysters (30-40mm) are sourced from the Channel Islands and are relaid in the Fleet for between seven months to a year. By this time they are of marketable size.

The superb water quality in the Fleet certainly plays its part. The sea waters flood in twice a day, mixing with the fresh water which runs into the river from the chalky Dorset streams. This contributes to the oysters' sweet and slightly salty taste.

An oyster is only as good as the water in which it grows and, by the same token, it's also a barometer of water quality.

Such detail might be superfluous to a customer, of course. Seated by the window with a view over the beds and the lagoon, they're more preoccupied with the delightful prospect of the best half dozen oysters they've ever eaten.

The oyster – part of our past

Oysters have a fascinating history in food culture. Famously reputed to be an aphrodisiac, they have yet to measure up to Viagra, or so my father-in-law says. These days, they are widely seen as an esoteric food.

It was not always so. In the 19th century, they were a staple diet of the poor, eaten in copious quantities. Beef and oyster pies and puddings were a classic Victorian dish and the poorer you were, the more oysters you put in. The richer folk could afford to add more beef steak to the dish.

Over time, and with changing farming methods, meat became less costly and oysters became the rich man's food.

At the Crab House we serve oysters au naturel. The classic accompaniments are a red wine and shallot vinaigrette and Tabasco but we do try other variations at different times of the year. It's a matter of personal taste – witness the American visitors who swore by a dab of ketchup with their oysters. The Crab House jury is still out on that one.

There is also a wealth of cooked recipes, such as Oysters Italiano with pesto and parmesan or Country Style with bacon and cream.

Either way, they're constantly in demand, which is why we have around 300,000 in various stages of development at any one time.

How to open an oyster

With a little practice, opening (or 'shucking') oysters will come as second nature.

First let's look at buying your oysters. Do as you would with mussels and first ensure all are closed. If any are not, it means the oyster is dead and should under no circumstances be eaten. The common practice of putting oysters on ice is not the best idea, since it will kill them, which is why we don't keep them that way at the Crab House.

If possible, try to buy direct from an oyster farm. You can then be certain of their freshness.

And so to the nitty-gritty. As Mrs Beeton didn't say, first take your knife.

You really do need an oyster knife, preferably one with a hand guard at the hilt, which is designed for this very purpose. It's short, with a thick pointed blade that does not have sharpened edges.

If you don't happen to have an oyster knife, it is possible to use a kitchen knife with a blunt but strong blade. But we wouldn't advise it. Better nip down to the kitchenware store on the double and get the right tool for the job.

Start by folding a thick tea towel in half. This is to protect your hand during the process. On a sturdy surface, place the oyster in the middle of the two halves with the hinged end still on show.

Now place your hand firmly on top of the tea towel, holding the oyster in place. Push the knife into the hinge of the oyster to a depth of about 2cm in, then twist the knife and the shell of the oyster should lift. Carefully run the blade of the knife along the back of the top shell to release the top shell. Discard this shell, then run the tip of the knife under the meat of the oyster to release it from the shell and it's ready to eat.

Best served with a slice of lemon, or a drop of Tabasco, or a drizzle of shallot vinaigrette to round it off.

To make the vinaigrette, simply combine the following:
1 shallot, finely chopped
200ml red wine vinegar

The Staff

Charlie

Visitors often ask what the specials are on a particular day. I would always answer that all the dishes are special. But yes, there are additional items on the blue board.

I can say that in all sincerity, having done my time in the kitchen as well as being front of house. We try to create something exceptional every time food leaves the kitchen for the table.

I love everything about the Crab House, whether it be demonstrating the hammer technique to those about to get to grips with the signature fresh crab or dodging the flying shell splinters as the diners joyously set about their task.

I could never tire of explaining new dishes and fish varieties that may be new to a customer. It's rewarding as it helps them make a considered decision. The same goes for wines, of which we have an extensive and varied cellar full.

For me, this is about more than just putting food on plates. Take for example the loaf of bread provided for each table. I like to see people breaking bread together. It's an age-old ritual heavy with meaning, a kind of unconscious bonding between families and friends.

Although for the time being I'm not involved in the day-to-day running of the Crab House, I will be returning at some point in the future. The café is truly a family project, with everyone contributing to its creation. We clad the building to look more like a wooden shack, landscaped the garden with boats and a few other fishing-related relics, and in summer it's brightened up with pink parasols and a hat stand – customers can borrow hats to keep the sun off them when they dine al fresco overlooking the Fleet and Chesil Beach.

Inside we kept it simple, with wooden tables and chairs and again a bit of fishing paraphernalia. A large open iced fridge cabinet displays the fish of the day for people to choose from. My grandfather did all the signs and we focused on making it a real family place where all ages could come and enjoy the food and environment. My mother Tracy takes care of all the finishing touches, such as fresh flowers in oyster shells on all the tables.

The menu changes all the time, sometimes twice a day, but we insist on the absolute freshness of the seafood we serve. It's not uncommon to see fishermen in their wellingtons coming through the restaurant straight from their boats carrying their most recent catch, but we wouldn't have it any other way.

Another thing that gives me great pleasure is to see children engage with the food. It may get messy when it comes to cracking crabs, but who cares? Adapting to new and different tastes is part of growing up, and if we can help this process along, so much the better.

That way, the next generation will still have an appreciation of good natural foods, even in an age dominated by processed and pre-packed products.

Long may that continue.

Charlie Bloxham

Dave

Our oyster farm is about two acres and has 20 rows of around 50 metres in length. This is all managed by my wonderful and spirited father-in-law David Scott.

A retired builder, he is a very keen fisherman and has been with us since we took over the oyster beds. He's a real godsend. He ensures that beds stay in good repair and that the oysters are progressing as they should and meet our quality standards. He can be seen regularly out on his raft tending to the oyster beds and lives on site during the week. He is always more than happy to talk to customers and explain the details of oyster farming.

There's never a quiet moment as we get through over 100,000 oysters each year in the café. David does everything by hand, including collecting, grading, washing and putting them through the purifying tanks. It is hugely labour-intensive, but we feel we offer the best oysters in the country. The flavour is fabulous.

The Essential
Ingredients

The fishmonger

Many of you reading this will not be fortunate enough to live by the sea and so not have ready access to a plentiful supply of freshly-caught seafood.

The next best thing is to have a trusted fishmonger – one who's always busy. You need to know that the seafood they are selling is fresh, and if they are not busy the stock will have been hanging around for too long. So for once, you should be pleased to see a queue in the shop.

We buy our fish from two or three different fishermen in the area. One is Ian Taylor of Seafood Naturally, who provides us with line-caught sea bass.

As the name suggests, line-caught fish are caught by a fisherman with a rod in his hand. It's the most eco-friendly and sustainable method of fishing there is – lines don't damage the seabed the way nets often can, and if the wrong species of fish is caught by mistake it can be returned to the water.

Use your common sense, as well as your senses, when buying seafood. It should look like it has just come out of the water. Fresh seafood will never ever smell fishy, but rather of the sea.

Once caught, the fish are killed humanely straight away, tagged and then immersed into an ice bath to kill any bacteria – all on the boat, whilst still at sea.

Ian really appreciates and looks after fish, which is an attitude that's very important to us here at the Crab House. Not only is his approach better from an ethical point of view, it also produces the very freshest fish – almost too fresh to eat. When they arrive at the restaurant, they're practically still flapping!

Use your common sense, as well as your senses, when buying seafood. To ensure the wonderful, delicate flavour and juicy texture of your seafood, you need to make sure it is fresh. It should look like it has just come out of the water. Fish should have bright, clear eyes. Smell is important. Fresh seafood will never ever smell fishy, but rather of the sea.

If you can find a good one, a good independent shop beats a supermarket every time...

Just good stuff

At the Crab House Café we have built a trusted network of local suppliers. This includes a couple of local bakers for our bread supplies.

When it comes to vegetables and eggs, we use Just Good Stuff at nearby Steeptonbill Farm, run by Steve Gould and Tess Evans. They run the business with a similar ethos to us: they aim to develop a mixed livestock farm that results in healthy, happy animals, reducing the food miles as much as possible to fit harmoniously into the rolling hills of North Dorset.

Steve and Tess supply us with their wonderful free-range eggs, all of which have yolks of a deep yellow colour with a superior flavour and quality that come in a range of colours depending on the breed of chicken.

Steve has had many years of horticultural experience. He started in a small way growing a great range of vegetables and selling at the produce auction at Wareham Market.

Today he and Tess take great pride in providing a range of produce that they have either grown themselves or traded locally with other small-scale growers. They have been running a small stall at weekends on Portland market for the past year or so, and the locals return again and again because they really taste the difference compared to the supermarkets.

We love visiting them at their farm, which overlooks the beautiful village of Milton Abbas. It consists of 15 acres of lovely south-facing pasture, a small wood and some farm buildings. It gives me great comfort and joy to know that our vegetables and eggs come from such a fabulous place.

Steve Gould and Tess Evans run their business with a similar ethos to us: they aim to develop a mixed livestock farm that results in healthy, happy animals, reducing food miles as much as possible.

Tamarisk Farm

We're fortunate that our corner of the country is filled with people with the same passion for great produce that we have. Arthur and Josephine Pearse of Tamarisk Farm are another couple who have that passion in spades.

The farm is just up the road from us in West Bexington, a beautiful site rented from the National Trust. Arthur and Josephine grow organic fruit and vegetables there, and the love and care they put into their work results in the most wonderful crops. That skill runs in the family too – their daughter runs a nearby chilli farm which produces the Dorset Naga, once the world's hottest chilli.

We mainly use Arthur and Josephine for their salad. They provide me with bags of leaves which always contain incredible treats like garlic chives, purslane and mustard leaves. I've never had a salad bag like it.

Arthur and Jospehine grow organic fruit and vegetables, and the love and care they put into their work results in the most wonderful crops.

They sell their wares to the public at the fantastic farmer's market in Bridport, which is a must-visit. Like all the local suppliers we use, the Pearses prefer the personal approach, and the small scale of their business means they offer great service as well as fabulous produce.

They don't supply to restaurants in a hurry, so we feel very privileged to be one of their customers. Josephine only lets me have six bags of leaves a week!

Here for the beer

A summer's day. You're seated outside under the pink parasols, the sun gleaming on the Fleet. What could be better than a refreshing glass of beer?

In case you're concerned that it's not the ideal partner to seafood, well, we'd thought of that. And we have created our very own Crab House Beer which goes down beautifully with dishes from our menu.

We have worked with Paul Walker of Hunter's Brewery to specifically develop a beer to complement seafood and shellfish – and it really is one of a kind.

Hunter's, based in Ipplepen, Devon, is a microbrewery and Paul uses only the finest Grade A materials, always striving to produce quality real ales.

Paul started out as a production engineer and then went into the sales industry. However, he found he was always away from home and corporate life was no longer for him. He pursued his dreams to start his own brewery after a bad day at work.

Hunter's Brewery was born out of some old buildings on a local farm and needed a complete makeover, and with help from family, friends and the community he was soon up and running. We are delighted to work with him and our customers love the beer.

Cheers Paul!

The view from here

Our restaurant looks out over the Fleet lagoon and Chesil Beach. The lagoon is an eight-mile stretch of saline water, which connects to the sea via a narrow channel at Ferrybridge into Portland Harbour.

Summer is of course the peak season for holidaymakers who come to Dorset. Come winter and other visitors arrive in their place, as the lagoon becomes home to thousands of Brent geese.

Chesil Beach (from the old English *ceosel* or *cisel*, meaning gravel or shingle) is 18 miles long. For much of its length it is separated from the mainland by the Fleet lagoon. And it's also surrounded by a mystery.

For reasons which still baffle scientists even today, the shingle varies in size along its length, from pea-sized at one end to pebbles as big as an orange at the other.

Indeed, legend has it that smugglers who landed on the beach in the middle of the night could tell exactly where they were by the size of the shingle.

My father-in-law David always jokes with customers that they can win £1million if they guess the number of pebbles on the beach correctly. It is said there are around 180 billion, so an exact figure may take some time to establish. Suffice to say so far he's had no takers.

It's a very well-known sailing area, and Wyke Regis provides an excellent viewpoint for events at the Weymouth and Portland National Sailing Academy, and in 2012 the sailing events of the Olympic Games. That was a great time for us, with many spectators calling in at the Crab House Café.

The South-West Coast Path passes around Wyke Regis village, which is around halfway along the Jurassic Coast and a dedicated World Heritage Site. The Jurassic Coast covers 95 miles of stunning coastline from East Devon to Dorset and features rocks that record 185 million years of the Earth's history.

World Heritage status was awarded due to the site's unique insight into the earth sciences, as it shows a geological 'walk through time' that spans the Triassic, Jurassic and Cretaceous periods. World Heritage Sites are places considered to be of 'outstanding universal value' and are selected by UNESCO (United Nations Education, Scientific and Cultural Organisation), which shows just how important the area all around the restaurant is considered to be.

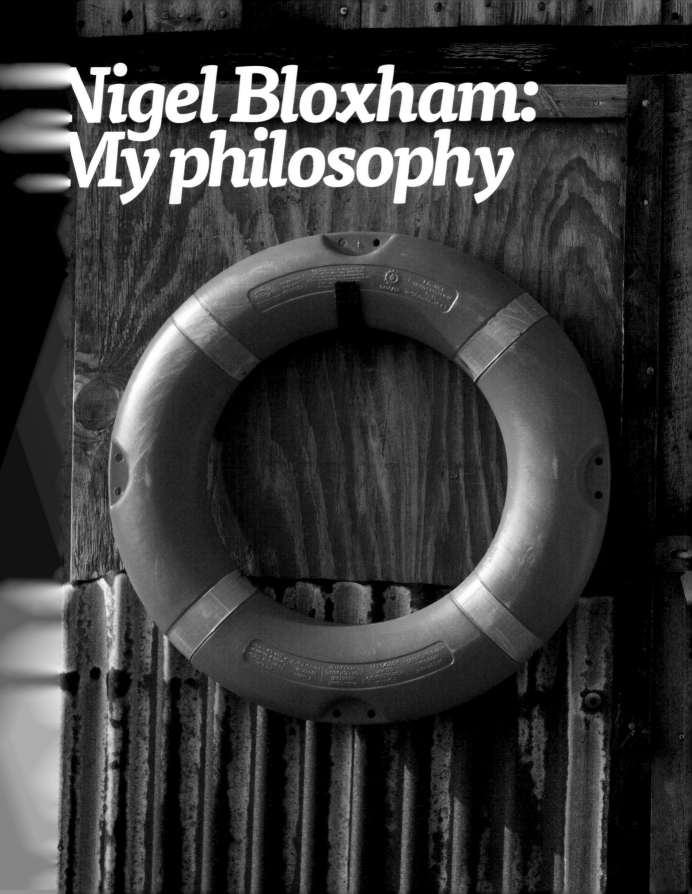

Nigel Bloxham: My philosophy

There's certainly never a dull moment at the Crab House Café. We get customers from all walks of life and there are lots of happy times and laughter.

It's a place where marriage proposals have often been made and the Champagne has flowed as everyone joins in the celebration. Then again, there have been one or two occasions where they've been turned down, which prompted a rapid retreat with the bubbly on ice.

On another occasion a customer told me proudly about how he had averted disaster by putting out a fire. It turned out the would-be hero, armed with a bucket of water, had snuffed out the smoker, complete with fish inside.

The reaction to our restaurant at every level has been overwhelming. It has certainly far exceeded my expectations. Praise has come from many national food critics and leading chefs.

Likewise, it is a source of great pride that diners come from far and wide just to seek us out.

I often wonder whether they're surprised when they turn the corner expecting to see a grand building, because their expectations have been built up by the press coverage. They quickly realise we're devotees of the early 21st century seaside shack school of architecture.

Yet everyone seems to take us as they find us. We're not about squashy sofas, rare antiques and expensive interior design. We just do what it says on the tin – the very best seafood to be found anywhere, cooked with care and skill in an informal, friendly environment.

When we created the Crab House Café I had in my mind somewhere I would want to come and eat and I am happy we have achieved this.

The praise from critics has also come in the shape of an AA Rosette, and listings in The Good Food Guide and The Michelin Guide, which we are delighted about.

As a Slow Food Ambassador, I am committed to the cause of Slow Food, a global grassroots movement that links the pleasure of food with a commitment to community and the environment.

This is what the Crab House ethos is all about. I am also a dedicated member of the Shellfish Association of Great Britain, which assists and promotes the sustainable development of the shellfish industry in the UK. I am very keen on giving back to the community and supporting charity. We are currently working with The

My message is never be scared to try something new in the kitchen - and there's no better place to start than with seafood. It offers so much variety and options. I'm always learning new things.

Fishermen's Mission to raise awareness and funds for this important charity that provides emergency support and practical care to fishermen and their families. We are acutely aware of the difficult life of a fisherman and have the utmost respect for them and their families. By way of doing our bit to help, we feature a charity dish of the day. Every time someone orders it, a pound will be donated to the Mission.

It is in my quest and desire to educate and inspire people about seafood that I have put together this book. Hopefully it will give you the confidence to have a go at cooking seafood and have fun doing it.

My message is never be scared to try something new in the kitchen - and there's no better place to start than with seafood. It offers so much variety and options. I'm always learning new things.

I also want to teach you about what to do with any leftover seafood: we always try and use up all parts. You can always make a fish stock – I have included some stock recipes for you to try. What happens if you have a glut of one type of seafood, and what's good at what time of year?

I know that for me Christmas is scallops time. I am a keen scuba diver and each Christmas Eve I go diving for scallops at Brixham, then go to the pub for a pint and then home with my scallops ready for Christmas Day.

I still love what I do and am looking forward to what the future holds.

Hopefully what we have done is bring great seafood to a wider audience, and this is what I want this book to do. It's my first book and through it I want to share with you some of the secrets and success of the Crab House Café kitchen. I hope you have as much fun and laughter creating our dishes in your kitchens at home for family and friends as we do.

Nigel Bloxham

Starters

Spiced sprats with sour cream and lime

Ingredients

1kg sprats (between 8-10 per person)

150ml double cream

170g flour – any type (you could use chickpea flour to make this dish suitable for coeliacs)

1 lime

30g curry powder

Oil, to cook

Milk, in which to dip the fish

Fresh chives, cucumber or red onion (optional)

Method

1. Squeeze the juice of the lime into the cream and briefly whisk. Chop the chives, cucumber or red onion into this if using. Leave it to stand in the fridge for 1 hour. Alternatively you could use shop-bought sour cream
2. Mix the flour and the spice/s to taste. If you don't like the idea of eating the heads of the sprats, remove them. One by one, dip the sprats in the flour, then the milk, then back into the flour. Shake off any excess flour
3. Fry the sprats in a deep fat fryer at 190°C until crisp. Drain on kitchen paper and serve with the sour cream

Chef's tip:

This dish is great with brown bread or a nice salad. You could also substitute the curry powder for Cajun spice mix, or a smaller amount of cayenne pepper (approx. 10g) for the classic 'devilled' fried fish.

Mussel curry

Ingredients

1kg mussels, washed and de-
bearded

500ml double cream or 285ml
coconut milk

½ glass of white wine

6 tbsp plain flour

Curry spice, either shop-bought
or your own

1 heaped tsp garlic and ginger
mix (see page 181 for recipe)

Method

1. In a saucepan with a good lid, fry off the curry spice on a high heat. Add the flour and the cream or milk. Add more flour if using milk

2. Pour the mussels into the pan with the wine and shake to help them to start opening. Put the lid back on to create the steam. Cook until they start to open

3. Once all the mussels are open, they are cooked. Take the pan off the heat, lift the lid and continue to thicken the sauce for a further 1 minute by stirring. Serve into bowls with some nice bread

Sea snails (whelks) with garlic and parsley butter

Whelks are arguably England's most valuable shellfish catch. In 2014, 720 tonnes was landed in Weymouth alone. But most of them go out of the country, mainly to Korea, where they're put in soy sauce, canned and sold as a bar snack. The Koreans believe they're good for the libido!

We wanted to encourage more people in this country to eat them, so at the 2014 Pommery (Champagne) Dorset Seafood Festival we launched the 'Great British Whelk Revival'. The campaign was so successful that we're running it again in future years, and we even managed to get the good ol' whelk some coverage in the national newspapers.

Whelks have got a bad name, because people remember them being sold on seafood stalls in the sixties and seventies where they were dried up, chewy and soaked in vinegar. But natural whelks are far tastier – they're big and fleshy, and as they're grown in the sea they have a lovely sweet, salty flavour. They're also environmentally friendly, because the pots used to catch them are almost always recycled.

Whelks have a natural sweetness, so they take spicy flavours like chilli particularly well – you can slice them up and put them in a stir-fry. This recipe is our take on escargot. Don't go to France for snails in garlic butter – join our 'Great British Whelk Revival' and eat them here instead!

Ingredients

2kg sea snails (whelks) with shells on or 500g shelled

250g garlic and parsley butter (see mixed herb butter recipe on page 174)

1 lemon

Salt, for cooking

Method

1. Take the whelks out of the shell
2. Bring a large pan of salted water to the boil, then add the whelks. Keep them just barely simmering for around 10 minutes. This cooks them right through
3. Take them out and drain. Slice them up so they don't look like whelks anymore, which is a good trick!
4. Fry the sliced whelks in a frying pan with a knob of the garlic and parsley butter. As soon as the butter has melted, squeeze the juice of the lemon over and serve

Chef's tip:

Sea snails are also nice with a root salad or slaw, but do serve some bread with them because you will want to mop up all that garlic and parsley butter. It may seem a lot of butter, but don't worry; just dunk your bread into it.

Razor clams with chorizo, broad beans and herb crumb

Ingredients

8 large or 16 small razor clams

170g chorizo, diced

225g cooked, peeled and husked broad beans

100g breadcrumbs

50g fresh herbs of your liking

100ml any oil

Pinch of paprika – if you like a little heat, substitute with cayenne pepper

Method

1. Steam the clams in a large lidded pan with enough water to cover for 2-3 minutes. As soon as they open, take them out. They might even be semi-raw but don't worry about that because they're going to get cooked again later. Roughly chop the clam meat. Retain the juice from the pot
2. Blitz the breadcrumbs and herbs together in a blender to make a herb crumb
3. Put the oil into a frying pan on a medium heat and add the chorizo. You're rendering down the chorizo and getting the oil to take on its flavour. It's done when it starts to change colour
4. Take the pan off the heat and add the paprika or cayenne pepper if using. Tip in the breadcrumbs and fry until they almost bubble and boil. Add the broad beans and just stir in
5. Add the chopped clam meat and pour in the juice saved from when you steamed the clams. Cook with the breadcrumb mixture until it starts to dry up
6. Spoon the mixture back into the clam shells on a baking tray and bake in the oven for 2 minutes at 200°C. It's very easy to overcook the clam at this stage. You're only really heating it – the crumb's already crispy and fried
7. Serve with lightly dressed salad leaves

Chef's tip:

Substitute the broad beans for peas if you prefer.

Toasted scallops with butternut squash purée and bacon bits

Ingredients

12-16 king scallops or 36-40 queen scallops

1 butternut squash

2 rashers smoked bacon or pancetta, chopped into lardons

Rapeseed or any other oil, to cook

2 tbsp fresh herbs such as dill, roughly chopped or 'picked', to garnish

Salt and white pepper, to season

Splash of double cream [optional]

Method

1. Cut the butternut squash in half lengthways, season it liberally with salt and pepper and drizzle a good dollop of oil on it. Roast on a baking tray in an oven set at 180°C until the flesh is soft and you can dig a spoon into it easily – this should take approximately 20-25 minutes

2. Let the squash cool slightly, get rid of the seeds and take the flesh out. Put the flesh in a blender, season with salt and plenty of white pepper. Blitz to a purée consistency. If you prefer a richer purée, add the splash of double cream

3. Put 1 tablespoon of oil in a pan and add the bacon. After about 1-2 minutes add the scallops. Cook for about 2 minutes on each side until nicely toasted

To serve:

Put a dollop of the butternut squash purée on the plate and make a smear of it by pushing the back of a spoon through it. Place the scallops on the plate and sprinkle the bacon bits over. We might also sprinkle a few green herbs, a bit of parsley for example. Our favourite is a little cutting of fennel

Chef's tip:

Ask your fishmonger for some broken scallops to use instead of whole ones. They are cheaper, and as they're broken they have more sides to toast and caramelise, which means they take on more of that great umami taste. You could also ask for roeless scallops, which are cheaper as well.

Old English potted crab and rustic toast

This is based on the age-old way of preserving food, which is to seal it in a jar with fat. Years ago you'd have potted all sorts of things. Fish, cheese, chicken, beef – anything really. You're sealing it in fat so the air can't get to it. We're going to flavour it so it's ready to eat. This is a good way of using up brown crab meat. You can put white meat in but I tend to leave it out because it doesn't really bring anything to the dish. We're going to need ramekin dishes, or I have done it in small glasses which looks nice, or little Kilner jars, which is how you see it in the picture.

Ingredients

250g brown crab meat
100g butter
¼ tsp mace
Pinch chilli powder (optional)
Bread of your liking, to toast

Method

1. Put the brown crab meat in a pan over a low heat and blitz with a hand blender. Melt the butter into it and add the mace, and the chilli powder if using. I suggest using a tad to flavour it, but not too much to make it hot
2. Once the butter has melted, pour the mixture into your ramekins, glasses or jars and let it set for a couple of hours
3. In the meantime, clarify some butter. I find the easiest way to do this at home is to put some butter in a jug and put it in the microwave for a couple of minutes, in 30 second blasts. Once melted, leave it for 5 minutes because it will carry on separating by itself. Leave it so the buttermilk and the butter oil split from one another. This happens when you put butter in a microwave to soften and you accidentally walk away and leave it, and it becomes a puddle. We've all done it!
4. Pour the clarified butter on top of the potted crab then put it back into the fridge for another couple of hours to set

To serve:
Toast your bread and spoon the mixture onto that. Serve some salad leaves on the side if you wish

Chef's tip:

This will readily keep for 7-10 days in the fridge. As well as having it on toast, you can put a spoonful over fish, like a herb butter. Pop the fish in the oven for one minute so the potted crab melts. Stir into some cream to get a nice crab sauce. Or chuck it in with some tomatoes to make a crab stew or sauce for pasta.

Raw cured sea trout with Waldorf style salad

Ingredients

1 sea trout, approx 450g

1 celeriac

1 Granny Smith apple

6 walnuts

2 tbsp mayonnaise

70g salt

30g white or demerara sugar

Juice of 1 lemon

Salt and pepper, to season

Bowl of water

English rapeseed oil, to dress

To serve:

When we're ready to use it, we slice it thinly onto the plate. We like to shave radishes onto it and serve with compressed cucumber, which is chopped cucumber that's been vacuum packed in some lemon and salt. We also like to put peppery flowers on – marigold works well, as do wild rocket flowers. Dress with rapeseed oil if desired

Method

1. First make the Waldorf salad. Our style is not the true Waldorf but we like it. Take the celeriac and chop it up into julienne or small baton shapes. Do the same with the apple, being sure to leave the skin on – it adds a bit of colour and texture. Squeeze the lemon juice into the bowl of water and drop the celeriac and apple into it to stop them browning while you make the rest of the recipe

2. Toast the walnuts on a baking tray in the oven at around 180°C for 2 minutes. You're only really warming them through. You might want to rub the skins off. I don't bother but it will be a sweeter nut if you do

3. Mix the apple and celeriac together with the mayonnaise. Season with salt and pepper. Crush the toasted nuts and use them to garnish when you plate up the dish

4. Make a salt sugar mix. Combine the 70g of salt with the 30g of sugar to make a curing mix. Put the fish on a wire rack over a baking tray and lightly coat with the mix. Cover with clingfilm – this will pull the water out and cure it. It can be left overnight, or you can do it in an hour, as that's when most of the curing takes place anyway

5. Once done to your desired time, pour away the juice, then wash the mix off the fish under the tap. You will notice the fish has firmed up

6. You now need to either hang the fish up or put it on a rack to dry. We need to dry it because that's what helps to preserve it. We don't want to put it in the fridge; too cold. You could speed up this process by patting it with kitchen paper, but really you want the air to dry it

Chef's tip:

If you've got a piece of sea trout left over, wrap it in clingfilm and put it in the fridge. It will keep up to a week easily.

Portland pearl oysters au naturel with all the trimmings

There are two types of oyster eaten in the UK – the Pacific (rock) oyster, available all year round, and the Native (or flat) oyster, which can only be eaten between 1st September and 30th April.

Oysters are bi-valve filter feeders and are usually cultivated and farmed in estuaries or sheltered waters. Devon and Dorset has some of the best conditions for shellfish cultivation and therefore produce some of the best grade oysters available.

Oysters may be eaten raw or cooked and have the 'taste of the sea' with a smooth fleshy texture. They are rich in Omega 3, copper, vitamin B12 and zinc. Zinc is used in the production of testosterone which may explain why they are considered an aphrodisiac!

Ingredients

6 oysters (Pacific or Native)

1 shallot

200ml red wine vinegar

2 sprigs fresh thyme

1 bay leaf

Tabasco sauce (optional)

Juice of 1 lemon (optional)

Method

1. Open oysters (see page 25) and arrange in a suitable dish, trying to keep them as upright as possible to avoid losing their liquid
2. Garnish with salad and lemon wedges
3. Serve with either a squeeze of lemon, a splash of Tabasco or shallot vinaigrette (see below)

To make the shallot vinaigrette:

1. To make the vinaigrette, put the red wine vinegar into a sealable container. Finely dice the shallot, chop the bay leaf and strip the leaves from the sprig of thyme
2. Add the diced shallot, bay leaf, thyme leaves and the remaining sprig of thyme to the vinegar. Add Tabasco to taste
3. Ideally, keep the vinaigrette in a fridge for a day to infuse. It may be used straight away or kept for up to a week chilled

Chef's tip:

Small segments of citrus fruits such as lime and grapefruit also work perfectly with oysters. We sometimes do 'tequila slammers' – lick some salt, eat an oyster and suck on a piece of lime.

Our sparkling Portland pearl oysters

Ingredients

12 large Portland pearl oysters
or whichever variety you prefer
or is available
2 tomatoes
2 banana shallots or red onions
Flour, to dust the oysters
1 tbsp oil
Salt, to season
Sugar, to season

Method

1. Boil a kettle full of water and pour into a bowl. Also fill a separate bowl with cold or iced water. Take the little core out from the top of the tomatoes – you can actually get a little gadget that does this for you now, and even as a chef I admit they're good! Nick the skin by putting a cut with a knife in the side, about 1 centimetre in. Put the tomatoes in a bowl of boiling water until you see the skin start to peel off, then take them out and plunge them into the cold or iced water. Take them out and peel them. They should peel really easily. Cut them in half, get rid of all the seeds then roughly chop
2. Finely dice the banana shallots by cutting them into strips one way then holding them in place and cutting them into dice the other way. Take your time
3. Mix the tomatoes and the shallots to make a concasse. Season with salt and sugar. You'll find that this will actually flavour the tomato and pull some of the water out
4. Meanwhile, open your oysters (see page 25 for instructions)
5. Take the meat out of its shell and roll it in flour. Put them on a plate ready for frying
6. Set up your oyster shells ready to serve. I make my oyster shell stand up by putting a pile of sand on a board or plate. It looks really nice. If you're by the sea you could of course have some seaweed, or failing that put it on some crumpled up paper, which will have natural holes to put the shell in
7. In a non-stick pan, heat 1 tablespoon of oil over a high heat. Put the floured oysters in the pan. Take them off once the flour is cooked, not necessarily the oysters – they may still be quite moist, but the protein in them has firmed up and tightened. This will probably take less then a minute

To serve:

1. Put a spoonful of the concasse into each oyster shell
2. Serve the oysters as soon as they are cooked
3. You can garnish with a sprig of herb. I like fennel, parsley and chive – anything green would show up really nice
4. Serve, enjoy, pour the wine. This is a good one for a nice buttery Chablis!

Portland pearl oysters with Dorset wasabi

Wasabi is a member of the Brassica family, which includes cabbages, horseradish and mustard. It has a unique sweet taste and a fiery heat which really wakes up the taste buds. It's native to Japan and has traditionally been eaten with sushi, but it's increasingly being used in all sorts of other dishes in Europe and around the world. We get ours from The Wasabi Company (www.thewasabicompany.co.uk), who grow it near here in Hampshire.

Ingredients

12 Portland pearl oysters, or whichever variety is available
100ml good quality shop bought mayonnaise
1 tsp fresh peeled grated wasabi

Method

1. Mix together the mayonnaise and wasabi
2. Shuck the oysters ready for serving

To serve:
Place the oysters in oyster bowls. If you haven't got any, you could place them in little piles of sea salt or chopped ice, both of which look quite nice (you could even colour the salt or ice with food colouring to add an extra dimension to the presentation)
Spoon half a teaspoon of the wasabi mayonnaise onto each oyster

Chef's tip:

If you like your heat, just grate fresh wasabi onto the oysters instead. We also chop up the stalks of the wasabi roots and sprinkle them on the oysters as a garnish – they've got a lovely crunch and flavour. You could add fresh horseradish for an extra kick.

Tangy smoked eel mousse with beetroot salsa

You can buy smoked eel pretty easily these days, at most good fish counters. We hot smoke conger eel. I find it makes a really velvety texture. With cream cheese you don't necessarily have to buy an expensive one. They all taste the same, especially when you're cooking or making dishes with it.

Ingredients

170g smoked eel
225g cream cheese
110g cooked beetroot
55g chopped red onion
1 tbsp balsamic vinegar
Zest of 1 lemon
Zest of 1 orange
Salt and ground black pepper

Method

1. Put the cream cheese in a bowl. Run your fingers through the smoked eel to flake it into the cheese – sometimes it has bones in it, which will need to be removed
2. Put the lemon zest into the bowl, and season quite liberally with ground black pepper. Put some salt in too, but not too much depending on how salty the eel is
3. Chop the beetroot and mix with the onion. Put the orange zest in – this just gives it a citrus hint and contrasts quite well with the lemon in the fish
4. Drizzle in the good old balsamic vinegar. Stir together to make the salsa

To serve:

We like to serve this rustically on a board with a bit of toast and some salad. We put a heap of it on there with a nice wedge of the lemon to squeeze on. It makes a nice spread or sandwich filling afterwards, so don't be frightened about making too much. It's good for canapé toast actually – a good party nibble. Grate fresh horseradish on top for a great taste and aroma

Huss salad with green beans and orange and nut dressing

Huss is a collective name for dogfish or what used to be known as rock salmon ('rock'). This is our twist on a niçoise salad really. This is the Crab House Café thinking outside the box. How many times are we told 'don't eat tuna'? Is it the right colour, bluefin, yellowfin, etc? Here we do it with huss instead – they can be buggers to skin, so ask your fishmonger to do it for you. But any firm fish would do – mackerel, bream and so on. I like the dogfish as it's under-utilised.

Ingredients

250g huss

200-250g green beans (runner beans, yellow dwarf beans or French dwarf beans)

4 hardboiled hen's, quail or duck eggs

8 tbsp orange and nut dressing (see page 178 for recipe)

250ml fish stock (see page 173 for recipe)

Splash of white wine or cider vinegar

4-6 walnuts, hazelnuts or cobnuts, to garnish

Method

1. Poach the huss in some fish stock, with a splash of white wine or cider vinegar, for around 15 minutes – have the temperature so the stock is barely simmering. Lift it out and let it go cold. If you leave it in, it will set like jelly
2. Blanch the green beans
3. Break the huss into large chunks and mix that in with the beans

To serve:
1. Dress the salad then serve a pile of the mixture on a plate
2. Add two halves of hardboiled egg
3. Put a nut on top along with a little extra dressing
4. If you wanted to you could have croutons with this, or anchovy fillets (as pictured)

Chef's tip:

My favourite serving suggestion is to deep-fry some small fish bones and crumble that on top – a sort of fish crackling.

Cockles and clams with tomato sauce and sea purslane

Sea purslane is becoming more popular – Waitrose sell it, for example. We pick our own right outside our doorstep. You could do this dish with just cockles or clams. When we've got both we mix them up together. Clams are certainly readily available in most big supermarkets or fishmongers.

Ingredients

500g clams

500g cockles

100ml basic tomato sauce [see page 173 for recipe]

50ml white wine

2 sprigs thyme

2 heaped tbsp sea purslane leaves [alternatively use marsh samphire]

Black pepper, to season

Method

1. Put a saucepan that takes a big lid onto a high heat
2. Add in the wine, thyme, a couple of twists of black pepper and the tomato sauce mix
3. Add the cockles and clams, put the lid on and steam until every one opens. Don't be afraid to pick the pan up and give it a good hard shake
4. The cockles and clams are ready when they're open, but before taking them out to serve we lift the lid off, chuck in the sea purslane and give it another 30 seconds on the heat before serving

To serve:
Serve in bowls, with some nice breads to dip in the sauce

Crab House fritto misto

'Fritto misto' means 'mixed fried fish,' so this dish can be odds and ends. You can buy mixed fish, or shellfish with the shells removed. The best thing to do is to get friendly with a fishmonger, go back so he knows you're a regular customer and say to him: "look, I only need 350g of mixed fish – have you got any trimmings you can let me have or save for me?" You may get a bargain.

Ingredients

350g mixed fish and seafood, including any of the following suggestions: John Dory fillets, squid, various shellfish (with shells removed), sprats

285ml batter (see page 175 for recipe)

250ml tartare sauce (see page 172 for recipe) or aioli (see page 176 for recipe)

Method

1. Coat the fish and/or shellfish in batter
2. Deep fry in batches in oil at 190°C. Take care to lay the fish/shellfish in the deep fat fryer slowly and away from you so no fat splashes up
3. Cook until the batter is crisp and golden to your liking
4. Serve with the tartare sauce or aioli for dipping

Oysters Italian style

Ingredients

6 Portland pearl oysters or
whichever variety you prefer or
are available
3 heaped tsp pesto (green or
red)
3 heaped tsp finely grated
Parmesan cheese
Salad to garnish

Method

1. Preheat the oven to 200°C
2. Place the opened oysters on an oven-proof tray, keeping them as upright as possible to avoid losing their liquid. Add half a teaspoon of pesto onto each oyster
3. Lightly sprinkle the Parmesan over all the oysters, trying to keep the amount even
4. Place in the oven until the cheese is golden brown (approximately 5-6 minutes)
5. To serve, place on a suitable dish and garnish with salad. Serve with rocket and vine tomato salad

Lemon pepper squid

Ingredients

1 large squid approx 6-8oz
(cleaned by fishmonger)
Juice of ½ lemon
2 tsp vegetable oil
2 tsp cracked black pepper
50g flour (optional)

Method

1. Slice the squid into small strips, no bigger than half a centimetre. Dust with flour for a crisper squid
2. Get your pan hot with the oil, until almost smoking. Carefully put the squid in and let it brown on one side. It will literally take 1-1½ minutes
3. Toss in the pan, squeeze in some lemon juice, a pinch of salt and your black pepper. That is probably the simplest, best thing you'll ever taste. You could mix it with an Asian-style salad

How to cook and pick a crab

Choosing your crab

White meat or brown? Everyone has their favourite.

Of course, there's no need to confine yourself to one or the other. But your choice of crab determines which colour meat you get most of.

The cock (male) tends to have larger front claws which contain more white meat, whereas the hen has smaller front claws, more of a domed top shell and generally contains more brown meat. The best way to tell them apart is by turning the crab over: the cock will have a much smaller centre piece compared to the hen.

Once you've decided that, there's the issue of how you are going to buy it. I would always recommend buying a live crab. This means you can control the cooking yourself, although lots of fishmongers will have pre-cooked crabs for sale.

Don't be afraid to ask if you can inspect a pre-cooked one more closely. In the hand, a good crab should have a distinct dense weight. You're not necessarily looking for the biggest on the counter.

But at the Crab House we take the view that live is always better. That's what we sell from our tanks.

Now if you're squeamish, here comes the tricky bit. You will need to kill the crab prior to cooking. You can take consolation in the fact that our way is the much more humane way as opposed to putting the crab into boiling water. It also prevents the claws dropping, a common occurrence with this method.

In case you were wondering, at the Café we have our own Crustastun machine. The machine passes voltage through salt water, which swiftly dispatches the crab: this is a very quick, effective, and deemed the most humane way to kill crustaceans (more information about the Crustastun machine and the process of stunning a crab can be found at www.crustastun.com).

At home, however, I would recommend that you put your live crab in the freezer for two or three hours, which will send it to sleep. Now it's ready for cooking...

Cooking your crab

Now for the cooking. This is very simple for an average-size crab of 1-1.2 kg.

Fill a saucepan with warm water from the tap, add a pinch of salt and then place the crab in a pan on the stove and bring to the boil. Simmer for around 15-20 minutes, depending on the size. Upon completion, remove from the heat and cool quickly under running cold water. Now you have the perfectly cooked crab. Easy eh?

I would always recommend buying a live crab.
This means you can control the cooking yourself, although
lots of fishmongers will have pre-cooked crabs for sale.

Picking your crab

Now, how to pick your crab: for this you will need:

• Three medium-sized bowls: one for the white meat, one for the brown meat and one for the shell
• A chopping board
• Either a crab pick or the back of a small teaspoon
• A large, heavy knife or hammer

Separate the large claws (1), pulling them away from the body and place to one side.

Next, separate the small legs from the body (2). To do this, hold the legs at the bottom on the thighs and lever out of the joint, pulling them at a 45-degree angle. Do this to all the legs. If one snaps and does not come out cleanly, use your crab pick or the handle of a small teaspoon to lever it out. Repeat this until all the legs are separated from the body.

Place the crab upside down on the chopping board with the main claws facing away from you (3). Now tuck your fingers under the small back legs, holding the top shell firmly down, then place your thumbs on the back of the main body of the crab and push up. This should separate the body and the top shell.

Now to remove the nasty bits! Some fishmongers will do this for you if you are buying a cooked crab so make sure to ask them. Otherwise, place the body and claws to one side and, with the top shell on the board, turn it 180 degrees: you will now see the front mouth piece again. With your thumbs, push this mouth piece firmly down and it should separate from the top shell (4 & 5). A small sac rather like a small plastic bag should come out with this: discard it all. In either side of the top shell is the brown meat. Scoop it out using a spoon and place it in one of the bowls (6). You can now wash the top shell out. This is perfect for presenting a crab salad or making a baked crab.

Next it's on to the body: this has gills, or as they are commonly known 'dead man's fingers', (7) all around it: to remove them simply pull them away and discard. Despite the name they are not life-threatening or poisonous, but simply tough and unpalatable.

The other bit to remove is the feather, (10) so called because it looks like a wet bird's feather. This is found towards the back of the crab.

Holding the body above a clean bowl and pick the meat out: this is the most time-consuming part (8 & 9).

You can now move on to those big claws that contain the premium white meat. Grasp the claw in both hands; lever it back against itself on the joint to break it into two pieces. Now, pick all the white meat out of the small section [11]. With the other piece of the claw, turn it over on the board until it steadies itself. Use either the back of a heavy large knife or a hammer sideways on and give the claw one hard whack [12]. Repeat this until you have a large crack in the claw. Pull the claw apart and pick all the meat out [13, 14 & 15].

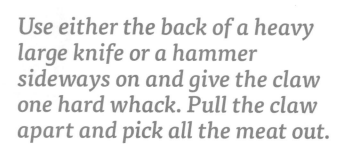

Do exactly the same for the other claw: be careful not to get any shell in the meat. I would recommend that after you finish picking the crab you lay the white meat out on a tray and check for any shell, as this can be rather unpleasant if eaten.

Use either the back of a heavy large knife or a hammer sideways on and give the claw one hard whack. Pull the claw apart and pick all the meat out.

Now for the smaller legs: take the smaller legs and break them back against themselves in the same way as the larger front claws. With the thigh part place it on the board and using either your hammer or back of the heavy knife crack just the end off. Use the pick or the back of the teaspoon to pick all the meat out [16 & 17]. With the smaller parts of the legs just smash them with the hammer/back of the knife and pick out the meat, avoiding as much shell as possible.

Top tip: Use all the leftover shell to make crab bisque/soup

Spicy baked crab

Ingredients

225g (8oz) brown crab meat (you can change this – all white meat or all brown meat, whichever you prefer but about 1lb in weight)

550g béchamel white sauce (see page 176 for recipe)

115g (4oz) grated cheese (Cheddar)

1 red pepper, diced

1 green pepper, diced

2 tbsp English mustard

2 tbsp chilli sauce or Tabasco

½ tsp Worcester sauce

½ tsp salt

Good pinch of white pepper

Method

1. Mix the cheese into the béchamel sauce along with the salt, mustard and Worcester sauce
2. Stir in finely diced red and green peppers, the crabmeat and leave to cool

To serve:
1. Fill either crab shells or scallop shells and place on top shelf of oven and bake until brown on top, about 12-15 minutes, and serve. A great supper dish with pitta bread and salad

The flyer you see in this picture is for the Fishermen's Mission. They're a very important charity for the world we're involved in – seafood. They provide emergency support to injured or shipwrecked fishermen, and financial and pastoral care to the families of fishermen who have sadly lost their lives. It's a really good cause close to our hearts. We often have dishes on the menu from which we donate one full pound per sale to the charity, and we also try to raise their profile by helping with fundraising events. You'll also find leaflets and donation boxes dotted around the Crab House Café.

For more information, visit www.fishermensmission.org.uk

Chef's tip:

Alternatively you could serve this on toast. If so, then put 2-3 egg yolks into the mix to help set, so it doesn't run off the toast. It can be piled quite thick. Heat and brown under a moderate grill for 10-20 minutes. Adjust chilli heat to suit. Again a great supper dish.

Spicy Chinese Crab

Ingredients

*4 freshly killed and cleaned
crabs – any variety that you
prefer or that are available
500ml ketchup – a value brand
will do
100ml white wine, fish stock or
water
2 tbsp Thai fish sauce
40ml light soy sauce
100g garlic and ginger mix (see
page 181 for recipe)
1 lemongrass stalk, finely
chopped or blitzed in a blender
8 spring onions, pared and
sliced lengthways
2 sliced peppers – red, yellow or
green
2 tbsp crushed dried lime leaves
125g fresh coriander*

Method

1. First make the sauce by combining the ketchup, garlic and ginger mix, lemongrass stalk, fish sauce, soy sauce and lime leaves in a blender until a sauce-like consistency has been reached
2. Pull the big claws off the crabs and take off the 'fingers'. If the crabs are particularly large, chop their bodies in half with a large knife or cleaver
3. Place the crabs, claws and fingers into a large saucepan on a medium heat and add the wine, fish stock or water to create steam. Add the sauce, reduce the heat to low and cook for 20-25 minutes
4. 2 or 3 minutes before the crabs have finished cooking, add the spring onions and peppers. You only need to heat these up so they stay crunchy like they would in a stir fry. At this stage also add the stalks from the fresh coriander (strip the leaves off to use for garnishing later), which will add an aromatic flavour to the dish

To serve

Garnish with the coriander leaves, dish up into soup bowls, put on a bib and attack!

Chef's tip:

Use pre-cooked crabs if you prefer – just reduce the cooking time to around 15 minutes.

Main Courses

Pan-fried sea bass with citrus fruits and coriander

Sea bass is a brilliant fish, very well-known and popular. We get it from summer right through to the end of the year. We insist on line-caught sea bass from local Weymouth fisherman, Ian Taylor. It's well worth the extra money, compared to the farmed sea bass that's around. Weymouth bass is tagged in the gills, so you know its identity and quality.

Ingredients

4 sea bass fillets (thick-end if possible), approx 175g each

1 orange

1 pink grapefruit

2 lemons

2 limes

100g butter, cubed

Coriander – a good bunch

A little white wine or lemon juice

A little rapeseed oil, or any type you prefer

Black pepper

Sea salt

Method

1. Firstly, with a sharp knife, slit the skin of the bass fillet many times
2. Rub or sprinkle a little salt onto the skin, leave to the side
3. Put a heavy non-stick pan on the stove to heat
4. Take the zest of the orange, lime, lemon and grapefruit and reserve in a bowl. Cut the top and bottom of each so they stand on the chopping board. Remove the pith by cutting down off the flesh. Segment the pieces and add to the bowl
5. Save the juice from the board then pour over the zest and segments (removing any pips)
6. Chop the fresh coriander
7. Oil the pan and place the fillets skin side down and cook for 4-5 minutes on a medium heat. Turn over the fillets – but only when the skin is crisp (it will not stick if it's crisp)
8. Once turned, cook for a further 4 minutes, remove, then add the citrus fruits, coriander, black pepper and any juice, or some white wine if you prefer
9. The liquid will bubble really quickly so lift off, put in the cubed butter and stir in. Keep stirring until the butter, fruit, juice and wine emulsify slightly
10. Adjust seasoning to your taste, then serve by spooning on the top of the fish and around the plate

Brill fillet with asparagus and hollandaise

Brill is often seen as the poor man's turbot. It looks very similar, although it doesn't grow quite as big. It's caught in the Channel and is a great fish to eat. We sell it a lot in the Crab House.

With brill you want to cook it fairly gently. So either you're going to cook it dry in the oven with a crumb that protects it or, as in this case, steam it. What you're really looking for is for the fish juices to mix with the white wine, which will create vapour in the cavity of the tray and foil, steaming the fish.

Ingredients

4 brill fillets, approx 175g each

12-16 asparagus spears

Hollandaise sauce (see page 177 for recipe)

½ glass white wine

Knob of butter or dash of oil

Salt and pepper to season

Sea purslane to garnish (optional)

Method

1. Place the brill fillets on a baking tray
2. Pour the wine over the fish, season it, and add the butter or oil
3. Snap the asparagus spears to where they break, or peel the bottom with a potato peeler. The woody bit is only on the outside – the inside is tender still
4. Put the asparagus on the tray beside the fish and then cover in foil
5. Place into an oven pre-heated to around 180°C for 10-12 minutes

To serve:

1. Put the fish and asparagus onto a plate, and spoon some hollandaise sauce next to the asparagus
2. Often we'll garnish it with some sea purslane, which gives just a slight saltiness to the dish. You could maybe have some new potatoes with it as well, but I really don't think you need a lot else

Chef's tip:

As an alternative, cook and serve this in a foil bag or parchment paper – as the French say, 'en papillote.' You could add theatre to your meal by opening it at the table. That way everyone gets the aroma, not just the cook. Make sure you don't put the hollandaise sauce in the bag when cooking as it would split.

Ling loin with salt beef and cream

Ling is a fantastic fish and I really like the slight chewiness of the flesh. Sometimes I describe it to customers as chewy cod, but that's probably being unkind and not doing it justice. It is of the same family as the cod and is often caught by rod and line over shipwreck sites; its favourite habitat is shipwrecks in the English Channel.

The fish is long and eel-shaped with a cod-like head but not as big. It can be a little tricky to fillet for the novice, so ask your fishmonger to fillet it for you if you prefer. The nicest piece is the loin, which is the fillet behind the head adjacent to the belly.

Ingredients

4 ling loin fillets, approx 175-225g each
250ml double cream
125g salt beef
½ white onion, sliced
½ tsp English mustard
Flour for dusting
Drizzle of rapeseed or any other oil
Salt and black pepper, to season

Method

1. Place the onion slices on a baking tray. Season the ling fillets and place on top. Drizzle with a little oil
2. Bake in the oven at 200°C for 10-12 minutes
3. Meanwhile, add a little oil to a pan and fry the salt beef until slightly brown. Pour in the double cream plus half a teaspoon of English mustard and simmer. Stir until the cream starts to thicken then keep warm
4. I love to serve this simply with carrots and peas and a little mash; place the ling on the mash, pour over the sauce and serve

Chef's tip:

If you wish to serve with chips, see our rustic chunky chip recipe on page 175 before starting. As an alternative, this dish is just as good with lots of green veg, particularly peas or broccoli. We have used wild foraged three-cornered leeks in the picture.

Mackerel escabeche, Dorset cider and apples

Ingredients

1.5kg whole mackerel

500g red onions

500g apples – any variety you prefer

1 litre apple juice

½ litre cider

½ litre cider vinegar

500g sugar

Star anise

2 cinnamon sticks

Bowl of milk, to dip the mackerel in

Bowl plain flour, to dip the mackerel in

Rapeseed or any other oil, for cooking

Salt and black or mixed peppercorns, to season

Method

1. Make a liquor by boiling the apple juice, cider, cider vinegar, star anise, salt and peppercorns, sugar and cinnamon until reduced by half
2. Simmer with chopped or sliced apples and onions for three minutes and then leave to cool slightly
3. Dip the mackerel into the bowl of flour, then the bowl of milk, then the bowl of flour again. Put into a frying pan with enough oil to cover and cook at 170°C until golden brown
4. Place the cooked fish on a plastic or ceramic tray deep enough to be able to cover the fish with the liquor. Don't use a metal dish
5. Pour the liquor over the fish and cover with clingfilm. Don't stretch the clingfilm tightly – just let it fall onto the fish and rest on its surface. This way the liquor will stick to the clingfilm and coat the whole fish
6. Leave to cool and place in the fridge for up to ten days
7. Serve with good bread to dip in the juice or as a lunch with new potatoes and a herb leaf salad

Chef's tip:

This dish is best served warm or at room temperature – don't forget to spoon the onions over the fish. A quick 'ding' in the microwave will warm it very quickly. The acidity of the vinegar helps keep the food safe to eat.

Lobster steamed with white wine, thyme, paprika, butter and finished with Somerset cider brandy

Killing lobsters humanely is a real talking point, isn't it? In the restaurant we've got our machine, the Crustastun (www.crustastun.com). I'm a big fan of it. We use it for our crabs and our lobsters. We put the lobster into salt water in the Crustastun, put the lid down, press the button and it releases an electric charge which stuns it, then an electric charge which kills it. It's really quick. And let's face it, we've been killing cattle this way for a hundred years or more, so why shouldn't we? What it means is that the poor old crab or lobster isn't trying to climb out of the pot, and we get beautiful, sweet, tasty, tender, juicy meat due to that fact.

Unfortunately it's not the sort of thing you'd have at home. So really I think the best and most humane way of killing a crab or lobster is to put them in the freezer for a couple of hours. They'll settle down and go to sleep almost as though it's a cold winter's day. It doesn't harm the flesh, it doesn't distort it and it doesn't bleed, which it would do if you put a knife into it in the wrong place, which is very easy to do unless you've done it many times before.

If you've got a lobster that's got a green or blue-green patch in it, don't be alarmed. This is the roe. It's very tasty and will actually turn bright red when cooked. It's what a classical French cardinal sauce is often made of. Certainly not to be thrown away.

Continued overleaf >

Ingredients

2 lobsters

1 tsp paprika

3 or 4 sprigs fresh thyme

4 tbsp or 'splashes' English Somerset cider brandy

1 lemon

1 glass white wine

Oil

1 knob of butter

Sea salt and black pepper, to season

Parsley, to garnish (optional)

To serve:

We always like to serve our lobster in a bowl so we put some of the sauce in there which you can dip with some bread. Garnish with parsley and a nice wedge of lemon – you've already used the lemon ends so nothing's wasted. Serve with a nice bit of salad and some good mayonnaise. It's also great with chips – our latest is sweet potato chips – or new potatoes if you're not a 'chippy' person!

Method

1. Once you have killed your lobsters (see previous page), place them on a chopping board, then cut them in half down through the middle and the tail. Remove the anal pipes or digestive tracts. Take out the 'bag' behind the heads. That's very important, because it will contain their last meal. It might be in one half or both, so please check

2. Take a large saucepan with a good lid and place it on the hob on a high heat. Put in a glug of oil

3. Sever the big claws from the lobster and whack them with the back of a knife. This is to enable heat to penetrate. Put the claws in the saucepan and put the lid on top. This starts to fry the claws. You get a strong umami, shellfish flavour – the same flavour you get if you barbecue a lobster

4. After about 5 minutes, take the lid off and put the bodies in with the claws. Add the paprika, thyme and a couple of lemon ends or wedges. I tend to use the ends because then I can use the rest for serving later on. Season with the salt and pepper then tip in the glass of wine. This will create the steam. Put the lid back on and turn the hob down to a low to medium heat. That's just enough for it to tick over and steam because you don't want the tails to go all tough and chewy. Cook for about 8 minutes, or 12-15 minutes for larger lobsters. If you have the luxury of a steam oven you can do it in that, but I find it easier and better in a pot

6. Meanwhile, flambé the cider apple brandy by adding it to a separate pan on a very hot heat. This burns off the alcohol, and by doing it in a separate pan it doesn't scorch the herbs that are in with the lobster

7. Tip the brandy in with the lobster and add the knob of butter. This will create a red syrupy sauce

8. Let it rest with the lid on for 4-5 minutes. This just lets it relax a little bit and makes for a greater infusion of flavour

Chef's tip:

If I haven't got cider brandy to hand, I tend to add some reduced apple juice to brandy to give it an apple flavour. You could also use calvados – but why, when there's fantastic English Somerset cider brandy available?

Whole sand sole poached in rosemary oil

This is my favourite way of cooking sole. Any type of sole will do, but sand sole, the true Torbay sole, is my favourite. The main result is very tender, moist flesh and surprisingly not at all oily.

Ingredients

4 large soles or 8 smaller ones
250ml olive oil and 250ml
rapeseed or vegetable oil, mixed
together
Fresh rosemary
1 garlic bulb, roughly sliced
Sea beet and potatoes to
accompany or just brown
buttered bread

Method

1. Ask your fishmonger to skin and trim the soles for you. You can use fillets, but I much prefer it on the bone as the meat seems sweeter and is really easy to eat
2. First, take the oil and put in a pan with a few sprigs of rosemary, you can, if you like, add garlic. Heat the oil very gently to 70°C, no more as you are not frying the herbs or fish. You can also do this dish in the oven if you want more control. You are basically gently poaching in oil. After about 30 minutes the oil will be totally infused. Now place the sole in the oil and keep the temperature between 65-70°C
3. You will notice after about 15 minutes the flesh will start to curl very slightly up off the bone. At this stage the fish is perfectly cooked, so lift out on to a plate and keep warm

To serve:
I love to serve this with brown buttered bread as a supper dish but it's also good served with sea beet that's been blanched then squeezed and re-heated in the herb oil with plain boiled potatoes. Plain and simply cooked – yum!

Chef's tip:

Don't be put off by this dish because of the oil – very little is left on the fish, it does not make it oily and a little of the oil on your bread or potatoes is just brilliant.

Megrim sole grilled with herb butter

Ingredients

4 normal-sized or 8 small whole
Megrim sole, skinned and
trimmed hard on the bone (ask
your fishmonger to do this)
4 knobs of herb butter (see
page 174 for recipe)
Plain flour, to dust the fish
Knob of butter or dash of oil
Salt and pepper, to season

Method

1. Pre-heat your grill to a medium to high heat
2. Lightly dust your fish with flour. This protects the fish and keeps it quite moist. Season it with salt and pepper
3. Coat a baking tray with butter or oil, depending on your preference. Place the fish on the tray and top each fish with a knob of the herb butter
4. Put the baking tray under the grill and cook the fish for about 6-8 minutes

To serve:

We serve this with salad or new potatoes. I quite like it just with some simple vegetables – some good mixed beans when they're in season. It's also good with peas. But these soles are so delicately flavoured and sweet that good ol' brown bread and butter is really all you need

Chef's tip:

We like to use rapeseed oil for cooking. There's lots of it around now, particularly English cold-pressed rapeseed oil. It's much healthier for you than sunflower oil. To use good olive oil for cooking is a bit of a waste, and it can burn. One of the things we do, however, is fill a bottle with about 20 per cent olive oil and the rest rapeseed oil. If you leave it for a day or two the rapeseed oil will take on the odours and characteristics of olive oil. It's a good way of stretching olive oil a bit further.

Steamed whole flounder 'Chinese style' with garlic, chilli, ginger and soy

A great fish, the flounder. It's found in the sea and in estuaries at certain times of the year. It likes fresh water and comes up the estuaries to breed. It's very popular with the Americans – they've got huge estuaries so they eat a lot of flounder. It's often considered a poor man's plaice. It's sometimes described as muddy in flavour, but I don't think it is. I think it's just a characteristic fish that's strong flavoured, and can take strong flavours with it like garlic, chilli and ginger. That's why we serve it Chinese style with some Chinese-style vegetables. It's great and very easy to do – a great supper dish.

Ingredients

4 whole flounder, approx 340g each

4 tbsp of garlic and ginger mix (see page 181 for recipe)

Mixed Chinese-style vegetables (this can be bean sprouts, mooli radishes, water chestnuts, shredded cabbage – whatever you've got around really)

1 glass white wine

Fresh chilli, finely chopped – how much you use depends on your preference for heat

1 lime, sliced

4 tbsp soy sauce

4 tbsp rapeseed or any other oil

Method

1. Pre-heat your oven to around 200°C
2. Place your Chinese-style vegetables on a baking tray
3. Score the flounder 3-4 times across the backbone. Put the garlic and ginger mix into the cuts you've made. Place the fish on top of the vegetables. Top the fish with the chopped chilli and slices of lime
4. Pour the wine over the fish and vegetables, wrap the tray in foil and put it into the oven. Bake for around 15 minutes

To serve:

1. While the fish is cooking, pour the soy sauce and oil into a bottle and give it a good shake to mix
2. Once the fish is cooked, use a fish slice to put each portion onto the plates. Put the fish slice under the thick, heavy end of the fish and pick it up along with the vegetables
3. Pour the soy sauce and oil mixture onto the tray, then pour this from the corner of the tray onto the plates as a dressing. The soy will split and make pretty patterns. This is great for dipping your fish into as you're eating

Chef's tip: *Try rice wine or sake instead of white wine.*

Sand dabs grilled with lemon and black pepper

Dabs are one of my favourites, even as a supper dish. They have a sweet, delicate flesh and are best cooked simply – I love them grilled with lemon, butter and pepper.

Ingredients

4 large dabs (or 8-12 small ones)
A knob of butter
1 lemon
Sea salt
Black pepper

Method

1. You can remove the skin as we have done in the picture, but it is fine to eat. If you're leaving it on, hand trim and top scale the fish so it is edible – you will need to scale the fish on both sides. Wash them under the tap after scraping the scales off to wash away the little ones you may have missed; these are tiny and not easy to see and not especially nice if you get a mouthful!
2. Rub the butter on a sheet of foil and place in a grill pan. Place the dabs onto the foil and add a further knob of butter to each fish. Squeeze on some lemon juice and then use the remaining pieces by stuffing into the gut of the fish carefully (you may have to cut into smaller pieces to fit a smaller fish)
3. Grind black pepper onto the fish to your liking and a very light sprinkle of sea salt (don't use if salted butter is used)
4. Put the pan under the grill, medium/hot, for 12 minutes and then back into the oven at 190°C for 10 minutes
5. Serve with vegetables or my favourite, brown bread and butter

Monkfish tail with garlic and rosemary

This is, I think, a classic. Monkfish tails can come in all sizes, from smaller ones right up to 2 or 3 kilos, although they would probably cost a fortune. If they're on the bone they're very easy to eat. You're not going to get any sharp bones stuck in your throat because there's only one through the centre.

To skin the monkfish tails, put a cut in the top and pull the skin back down over it. Between the skin and the monkfish tail itself is also a membrane. If you don't get rid of that it can be a little bit rubbery and sinewy, and become tight like an elastic band. It has a blueish purple hue. Make sure you remove it, or better yet ask your fishmonger to skin the monkfish tails and remove the membrane for you.

Ingredients

4 monkfish tails 250-300g each
½ white onion, sliced
250ml roast garlic oil (see page 179 for recipe)
2 lemons
5 sprigs fresh rosemary
Salt and pepper, to season

Method

1. Pre-heat your oven to about 220°C
2. Cut either side of the bone down the thick end about halfway down the fish. This will create a piece of flesh that looks a bit like an ostrich foot. The idea of that is that it will cook a lot more evenly. For the same reason, score the back of the fish. This also helps to let the heat in
3. Put the sliced onion onto a baking tray to act as a trivet and stop the fish sticking to the tray. Add a sprig of rosemary and place the fish on top. Squeeze the juice of one of the lemons onto the fish and place the lemon skin under and around the fish to infuse. Season with salt and pepper and drizzle with the roast garlic oil
4. Put the tray into the oven and bake for about 12 minutes
5. Take the tray out, cover it with foil and let the fish rest for 5-10 minutes. This is a meaty fish – you need to let it relax

To serve:

This is a great one to serve simply with lots of new potatoes or a good tomato salad. A good wedge of lemon is always good when you've got oil and garlic, and you could also garnish with a couple of fresh rosemary sprigs for that extra finishing touch. Then what else do you need other than some bread?

Chef's tip:

This dish is nice to eat cold as leftovers too. Mix the fish with a bit of mayonnaise and have it on some toast. In fact you could do this with any leftover cooked white fish. Garlic + mayo + seasoning to taste = a great snack dip.

Hake fillet steamed over tomatoes with olives and saffron potatoes

Hake's a great fish, and often reasonably priced to buy as well. The Spanish eat loads of it. Most of the fish caught on these shores is sold to Spain, which I think is a great shame. It can be a bit soft if you're not buying from a reputable supplier, but when it's relatively firm it's a lovely fish. You can do all sorts of things with it. We're going to do it here with tomatoes, olives and saffron potatoes in one pot on the stove.

Ingredients

4 hake fillets, approx 225g each

4 potatoes (King Edwards or Maris Piper)

200ml basic tomato sauce (see page 173 for recipe) or shop bought equivalent

Orange zest

115g (4oz) black and/or green olives, drained

½g saffron

200-250ml fish stock (see page 173 for recipe)

Sea salt and black pepper, to season

Method

1. Peel the potatoes and cut them into cubes of around 1 centimetre, then put them in a large saucepan. Pour in the fish stock to cover the potatoes, add the saffron and season with the salt and pepper. Par-boil the potatoes
2. Add the tomato sauce to the par-cooked potatoes and put in the orange zest. This will give the tomatoes a real zesty Spanish flavour
3. Place the hake fillets onto the potatoes and tomatoes, put the lid on the saucepan and steam on a low heat for around 20 minutes

To serve:

1. Check the fish is cooked then take it out onto a tray. I suggest you then ladle out the potatoes and tomatoes into bowls and place the fish on top
2. You can garnish with some fresh herbs – whatever you have available

Chef's tip:

Quite often we chuck in some sea purslane at the last minute to steam. We also put sea beet in sometimes. The nearest equivalents are spinach or marsh samphire.

Smoked haddock white bean cassoulet (stew)

My fish version of the classic French cassoulet. We had one of our wine suppliers over from France and they were knocked out by it. They couldn't believe you could do this iconic dish by reworking it with fish. Smoked fish is often salty, and the French do their cassoulet with salty pork so I'm getting the same salty flavour. It's almost like a bean chowder I suppose, thick and creamy. The beans soak up all those nice flavours.

Ingredients

350g smoked haddock

450g white beans

Milk, enough to cover the fish

Fresh mixed herbs – whichever varieties you prefer, such as Provençal, bay leaves or parsley

Method

1. Soak the fish in milk for 3-4 hours, or overnight if possible. This makes the fish less salty
2. Poach the fish for 3-4 minutes in the milk it has been soaking in. Remove it from the pot and place on a tray or plate ready to be flaked up and put into the stew later
3. Add the beans to the milk and cook in the oven at about 190°C for between 45 minutes and an hour. The starches in the beans will come out and thicken the milk into a stew-like consistency
4. Flake the fish into the stew and add the herbs. Cook for a further 15 minutes

To serve:

This truly is a peasant's dish. So what else do you need other than some good crusty bread?

Cod fillet with black pudding crumb and poached egg

They keep telling us 'you shouldn't eat or buy cod.' But if the fisherman has caught cod as a by-catch, I'll serve them on my menu. There is no sense in wasting them. There seems to be more cod in the Channel than there ever was ten years ago, in much better condition. They tell us to eat Pollock or ling instead. I'm not a scientist but if we all went out and only ate ling, there'd be a shortage!

I'm not for or against cod. What I'm really saying is we shouldn't just eat cod. We should eat other fishes because they're bloody good to eat too. And I hope this book demonstrates that!

As for the breadcrumbs, make sure you save your crusts of bread. We don't throw anything away in the restaurant kitchen – a penny saved is a penny gained! To make breadcrumbs the bread needs to be stale. You could shove it on a tray in the oven after you've finished cooking to dry it out. Once it's dry or stale, blitz it in a blender. Far better than any shop-bought breadcrumbs.

Ingredients

4 cod fillets, 200g each

115-170g (4-6oz) black pudding, chopped

½ white onion, sliced

4 eggs

225g (8oz) breadcrumbs

1 tbsp of rapeseed oil or any other oil

Salt and pepper, to season

Method

1. Put the breadcrumbs and chopped black pudding in a blender with the oil and pulse until you have a black crumble
2. Poach the eggs to your liking, then 'refresh' by plunging them into a bowl or pan of ice water ready to be re-heated in the oven later
3. Pre-heat the oven to around 210°C
4. Place the onions on a baking tray. Lay the cod fillets on top of the onions and season with the salt and pepper. Cook in the oven for 6-7 minutes
5. Take the cod out of the oven and cover it with the black pudding crumb.
6. When the crumb is starting to brown, take the tray out of the oven again. Place the poached eggs on the tray and return to the oven for 1-1 ½ minutes

To serve:
I like to serve this with peas or beans – nice green vegetables. It would also work well with bubble and squeak

Chef's tip:

Substitute the green vegetables for roasted tomatoes to complement the egg and black pudding and make this dish a fishy twist on a full English breakfast.

Pouting fish and chips in light beer batter

Pouting fish is a member of the cod family. It has the familiar 'beard'. It's sometimes also known as bib. It's a fish that doesn't tend to be worth much on the marketplace. Fishermen don't tend to look after it as much which is a great shame. It doesn't keep as well as cod so the quicker you can get hold of it the better. I prefer it skinned but it doesn't hurt to leave the skin on. If you go to Scotland, fish and chips is haddock, and skin-on every time. You could do it with small hake as well. But the most sustainable is pouting. It's an underused fish, and we should use it more.

Ingredients

4 pouting fillets, 200g each
550ml beer batter (see page 175 for recipe)
Plain flour, to dust the fish
Rustic chunky chips, prepared as per recipe on page 175
Salt and pepper, to season

Chef's tip:

For the coeliacs amongst you, use chickpea flour (gram flour) to make the batter wheat-free. For an extra crunch, put a couple of spoonfuls of rice flour in with it.

Method

1. Lightly coat the fish with salt and leave it for half an hour. This just pulls out some of the moisture and firms up the flesh. Wipe off the salt and pat it dry with kitchen paper
2. Par-cook the chips in a deep-fat fryer as per the recipe on page 175. Remove the chips and the fryer basket and place to one side
3. Turn the heat up to around 175°C ready to fry the fish. Season the flour then use it to lightly coat the fish by holding the tail or the thinnest part of the fish with your fingers pinched and dipping it in the flour. Next, dip the fish in the batter so it coats. Pull it out of the batter and let it drain a bit. You might need to wipe it on the side of the batter container. Next time you go to the chippy, watch them do it!
4. Gently sink the coated fish into the fryer. Don't drop it because it will splash, and you could burn yourself or splash batter onto a flame. It's easier to fry it in the fryer without the basket because often the batter can stick to the basket
5. When the fish is cooked, after about 6 minutes, it will float. It may pop up too early because of air in the batter, in which case you might need to turn it over. Use a slotted spoon to take it out when it's cooked, and put it onto some kitchen paper to drain and keep warm
6. Turn the oil up to around 195°C and lower the basket and chips back into the fryer. Cook until crunchy and golden, or to your liking

To serve:

Get your lemon, vinegar, tartare sauce or mushy peas. There isn't a lot else you need with this traditionally. But you could do a modern take on fish 'n' chips like we do at the Crab House Café. Overleaf you'll find the things we do here to jazz it up and bring it into the 21st century

Cauliflower purée

Ingredients

1 medium-sized cauliflower
3 tbsp curry powder – mild or
hot, depending on your
preference
1 tbsp rapeseed or any other oil
Salt and pepper, to season
85ml of cream or milk (optional)

Method

1. Boil the cauliflower in a pan of water until it becomes soft
2. Meanwhile, heat the oil in a pan on a low-medium heat. Add the curry powder and fry it off for 1-2 minutes to bring out the flavour
3. Once the cauliflower is cooked, drain it and put it in a blender. Season, add the fried curry powder and blitz to your preferred consistency
4. If you like a smoother, richer purée, add cream or milk while you're blitzing until it reaches a custard-like consistency – the technical term is 'the ribbon stage'

Chef's tip: *To make this dairy-free, use coconut or soya milk*

Cucumber dill

Ingredients

1 cucumber
2 tbsp fresh dill

Method

1. Finely chop the dill. Peel the cucumber and roll it in the dill
2. Cut the cucumber into slices or chunks and serve

Beetroot pickled egg

Ingredients

1 cooked beetroot
1 jar pickled eggs

Method

1. Add the beetroot to a jar of pickled eggs and leave it for a week. The eggs will turn pink

Thai fish curry with cabbage and fragrant coriander rice

Ingredients

700g fish such as coley,
monkfish, ling, huss, conger eel
500g shredded cabbage –
green, English pointed or white
depending on your preference
200g of long grain or basmati
rice
Half a preserved lemon (see
page 180 for recipe)
1 tbsp of garlic and ginger mix
(see page 181 for recipe)
Chopped red, green or yellow
chillies – how much you use
depends on your preference for
heat
1 heaped tbsp of Thai paste –
green, red or yellow depending
on your preference
2 cans coconut milk, or 1 can
coconut cream and 1 can dairy
milk
1 stalk lemongrass, chopped
1 large bunch fresh coriander
1kg leeks (optional)
1 small bunch spring onions
(optional)

Any meaty fish is good for this. You can get the Thai paste from any Asian shop – much better than the Thai sauce often found in supermarkets. Do taste as you go along, because it can be quite hot. The Asians have a different heat tolerance to us. Thai food is also really fresh, so this is almost like a hot crunchy salad.

Method

1. Cook the rice as per the packet instructions. Once cooked, add the preserved lemon and half of the chopped coriander and leave this to infuse
2. Put a large saucepan on the stove over a medium to high heat. Add the Thai paste, garlic and ginger mix, chillies, lemongrass and the rest of the coriander. Pour in the coconut milk, or coconut cream and dairy milk. Bring to the boil
3. Add the shredded cabbage, and leeks and/or spring onion if using
4. Add the fish, and season the pot with salt and pepper
5. Cook fairly rapidly, about 5-6 minutes. Once the fish is cooked, the vegetables will be too. You only really want to warm them

To serve:
Serve in a big dish with the fragrant rice. It's also good with a bit of lime added. This is big on flavours

Chef's tip:

Don't be frightened to add your own ingredients. You could always add some green beans – the Thais put a lot of those into their food. Make the sauce as thick or thin as you like.

Huss pan-fried and stewed in red wine gravy with bacon, thyme and paprika – see the recipe on the next page

Huss pan-fried and stewed in red wine gravy with bacon, thyme and paprika

This is a great meaty dish – a good dish to convert a meat-eater to fish, as it is essentially a meaty sauce.

Ingredients

1kg huss/dogfish

150g bacon lardons

200ml red wine – use the red wine you are going to drink with the dish if you can. A cabernet shiraz, merlot or zinfandel would be good.

Seasoned flour for dusting

1 tbsp paprika

2/3 sprigs of thyme

2 tbsp cooking oil

125g unsalted butter

Salt and pepper, to season

Method

1. Ask your fishmonger to cut the huss into 20 millimetre thick steaks across the bone (the bone is easy to cut with a sharp knife); it is only a round backbone which makes it an easy fish to eat
2. Put the flour and seasoning into a bowl. Add the fish steaks and turn over to coat. Keep to one side
3. Take a large frying pan and put in some oil and start to fry the bacon lardons over a medium-hot heat. Move them to one side once browned
4. Place the fish steaks in the pan. Fry for 2 minutes, turn and fry for a further 2 minutes – add more oil if the pan is dry or burning. Turn down the heat to medium, sprinkle in paprika and the stripped thyme leaves then pour in the red wine and simmer until it starts to thicken
5. Taste and season with a little salt and pepper (it may not need salt due to that in the bacon). Take the fish off the heat and out of the pan
6. Stir in the butter cubes and keep the sauce in the pan moving. This will thicken and enrich the sauce and make it shine – if the pan is too hot the butter and oil will separate, which you don't want to happen. If it does, then add 3 tablespoons of cold water and stir vigorously. It should pull back – you could also add an ice cube
5. Serve immediately onto warm plates with roasted winter vegetables or potatoes of your choice

Spicy octopus stew

At different times of the year, both in Scotland and down here in the south, you get catches of small octopus. They find it in the pots and nets. The octopus is the single sucker and is seen as the lesser octopus, not like the ones you get in the Mediterranean. Those are thought to be much better eating, but they are very, very expensive. We tend to freeze the octopus first, then defrost it, clean it, cut it up into rough chunks, then freeze it up again. What this does is actually start to tenderise it by breaking down the muscle cells.

Ingredients

1 octopus

Basic tomato sauce (see page 173 for recipe) or shop-bought equivalent

Salt and pepper, to season

Method

1. Defrost the prepared octopus and chop into chunks of roughly 2 centimetres in size. Add this to a slow cooker or casserole dish
2. Pour over the tomato sauce and season with salt and pepper
3. Cook in the slow cooker or in the oven on the lowest heat setting possible for a minimum of 6 hours. You've got to cook it for a long time to get it nice and tender. It gets to a stage where it tightens then relaxes, releasing all the juices

To serve:
1. Taste, and adjust the seasoning to your liking
2. Serve with vegetables of your choice, or potatoes, or just good bread

Chef's tip:

Add some olives or orange zest to the tomatoes to give the dish a nice twist. You could also roast the octopus off on a tray with some oil before you add the tomatoes for extra flavour.

Black bream baked in fragrant salt

Fragrant salt is best made a few days beforehand. I really like this idea. You can do it with any fish really but I think it particularly suits the oily bream very well. A great family-style party dish.

Ingredients

4 whole black bream, approx 450g each

3kg rock salt

2 heaped tbsp black or green peppercorns

4 egg whites

Herbs, spices, fruits and vegetables of your choosing to flavour the salt

Method

1. Put the salt into an airtight container. Add to this any herbs or spices of your liking. For example, you could go down an Asian-inspired route, with fennel seeds and star anise, or the route which I quite like, which is lemon and lime zest. That gives off an aroma that you wouldn't believe. Don't forget to put some peppercorns in too. Leave it 2 or 3 days and when you lift the lid you'll get the most amazing smell
2. Lay a sheet of foil out onto a baking tray. Mix the salt with the egg whites and spread half of it onto the foil. You can do without the foil but I think it's easier and cleaner with it
3. Put the fish onto the salt. Stuff the belly or cavity of the fish with whatever you want to flavour it with – a lemon or orange, a bulb of fennel, some herbs. Then cover the fish with salt. The idea is to seal it in
4. Fold up the foil around the sides so it holds the fish together and the salt on the fish. Bake for 25 minutes in an oven set to 200°C. The fish almost steams inside

To serve:

1. In the restaurant, we tend to serve it with the foil rolled down. We give the customers a hammer to break the hard salt with and a bucket to put the salt into. You get these wonderful smells when you take it to the table. Unusually you can cook this fish with the scales on because the skin will come off stuck to the salt
2. Serve with boiled potatoes. Although I promise the fish won't be salty, there is a slight sea-saltiness to it, and potatoes complement salty food nicely. Alternatively you could serve with a potato salad, or maybe some salad leaves. But the fish is the star. It's the fish that you're eating, so you don't want too much else

Mackerel stuffed with feta cheese and beetroot

Ingredients

4 large or 8 small whole
mackerel

170g beetroot

110g feta cheese

170g breadcrumbs

½ white onion, sliced

1 orange

A dash of English rapeseed oil

Plain flour, to dust the fish

Salt and pepper, to season

Method

1. Gut the mackerel, leaving the heads on but taking the gills out. Score it 3 or 4 times along the thick 'shoulder' end, making the cuts less deep as you go all the way down. It looks really pretty, but it also allows the heat into the fish and means that the tail won't cook before the thick end has

2. Take the beetroot. This can be any type – all the heritage beetroot that's around now is really nice – but I tend to like the good old dark red beetroot for this dish. Using your hands, mash it up in a bowl with the cheese and breadcrumbs until it's all worked in together. If you're worried about coeliacs you could leave the breadcrumbs out, although that makes it a bit harder

3. Stuff the mixture into the cavity of the fish with a wedge of the orange. Also put some orange peel into the head of the mackerel

4. Season the flour, then roll the fish in it

5. Put the sliced onions on a baking tray and place the fish on top. Drizzle with oil

6. Put into the oven at 220°C and roast it for around 8 minutes, until the skin is hard and crisp and golden. To check that it's cooked, you can put your knife in just behind the head, and if the flesh comes away from the bone it's done. If it's nearly there take it out and let it rest – it will carry on cooking through the middle

To serve:

I think it's best served with salad. It's quite a summery dish. A nice little bean salad or a good rocket salad – something like that would be good, with a nice lemon or orange dressing on it. Orange zest and French dressing would be great, and toasted hazelnuts. Any toasted nuts would finish this dish off nicely. It would also be great on a Middle Eastern-style couscous

Turbot poached with sea beet and mussels

Turbot is the king of fish. It's one of the bigger fish and certainly the most expensive. You can find smaller ones now – the big ones tend to go abroad. They're caught from March onwards, through to October time. It's a thick fish and we often steak it up, which means we're cutting it on the bone. Your fishmonger can do this for you. We're putting it with sea beet, which we forage along the coastlines. When asked to describe sea beet by my customers, I say it's like leathery spinach, but don't let the 'leathery' bit put you off! What I mean by it is it's thick and fleshy and doesn't disintegrate in water. If you can't get sea beet of course you can use normal fresh leaf spinach.

Ingredients

4 turbot steaks, 250-300g each

220g sea beet or spinach

500g mussels

4 tbsp double cream

50ml white wine

200ml fish stock [see page 173 for recipe]

Salt and pepper, to season

½g saffron (optional)

Method

1. Take a deep saucepan with a lid and place on a low heat on the stove. Put the turbot steaks in the pan, add the wine and fish stock to create steam and put the lid on
2. After 12-15 minutes depending on the thickness of the fish, take the pan off the heat, lift the lid off and take the dark skin off the turbot steaks. Put the fresh mussels in their shells into the stock, along with the double cream, the sea beet and saffron if using, and return to the heat for a final 5 minutes. If you're using spinach, just stir it into the stock to wilt at the end instead
3. Return to the heat for a further 5 minutes. Taste, adjust seasoning and serve

To serve:

I like to serve this dish in a bowl, with potatoes and green beans or asparagus. Leeks and carrots would also work well. I don't think there's anything that wouldn't work with this to be honest. Put the vegetables in the bowl, put the fish on top and pour the mussels and sauce over it. Happy days

Gurnard fillet green tandoori style

Ingredients

4 pin-boned gurnard fillets, approx 180-200g each

250ml base curry sauce (see page 172 for recipe)

½ onion, sliced

6 chopped green chillies, or more if you prefer more heat

150ml Greek yoghurt

150-200g basmati long grain rice, or more if you wish

2-3 wedges preserved lemon, finely diced (see page 180 for recipe)

225g coriander (200g for the green tandoori sauce, 25g for the rice)

100g mint leaves

4 tbsp rapeseed oil

1 tbsp garam masala

2 tsp salt

Method

1. Take the gurnard fillets and feel them to check that all bones have been removed. Put the fillets in a bowl with base curry sauce, coat and cover with clingfilm. Don't stretch the clingfilm tightly – just let it fall on the fish and rest on its surface. This way the sauce will stick to the clingfilm and coat the whole fish
2. Put the bowl in the fridge and leave the fillets to marinate for 2 hours
3. To make the green tandoori sauce, blitz together the mint leaves, chillies, oil, salt, garam masala and 200g of the coriander in a blender. Fold in the yoghurt
4. To cook, pre-heat the oven to 220°C
5. Place the sliced onions on a baking tray and drizzle with oil to stop the fish sticking. Take the marinated fillets out of the fridge and place them on top of the onions. Spoon the green tandoori sauce on top and bake for 8-10 minutes

To serve:

1. Cook the rice as per packet instructions or however you normally would, and refresh
2. Chop the remaining 25g of coriander
3. Mix together the rice, coriander and finely diced preserved lemon wedges in a bowl. Cover with clingfilm and microwave on full power for 2 minutes. Let stand for 1 minute, then microwave on full again for 1 minute. While reheating the rice steams itself, infusing it with the flavours of lemon and coriander
4. Serve the rice with the cooked gurnard fillets and some flat bread

Chef's tip:

Any leftover rice could be served cold as a salad with French dressing.
Do not reheat the rice.

Chunky haddock fillet with wild mushrooms

Our wild mushrooms are not technically wild. They're wild varieties cultivated. There's lots of mushroom picking going on now and people who don't know what to look for have ended up being very ill. A couple of cases have been serious enough to lose their lives. We don't trust wild foraged mushrooms. It's my duty to serve safe food to the customer. We get most of ours from a lovely company called Fundamentally Fungus (www.fundamentallyfungus.com), who are not a million miles away from us in Stockbridge, Hampshire. They will supply households as well as chefs, so look them up. The mushrooms they have in supermarkets are pumped full of water. There's no flavour! When I first tasted Fundamentally's wild mushrooms I couldn't believe the difference. They don't shrink in the pan. You can do all sorts of different things with them. They are seasonal – some grow through the winter months, some through summer. In this dish we like to mix up the varieties. Abalone is usually one of them – it almost tastes like beefsteak.

Ingredients

4 haddock fillets, approx 280g each
200g wild mushrooms [approx]
½ white onion, sliced
Flour, to dust the fish
Rapeseed or any other oil, for cooking
Knob of butter
Salt and black pepper, to season
2 sprigs of thyme [optional]

Chef's tip:

Mushroom ketchup can enhance this dish. It's an old-fashioned English condiment. You see it in supermarkets next to the anchovy essence.

Method

1. Skin and pinbone your haddock fillets, or ask your fishmonger to do this for you
2. Lightly dust the fillets with flour and season with salt and black pepper. Fold the tail in under or over the thick bit of the haddock, then make an incision so when cooking it doesn't uncurl. You could fold it 2 or 3 times. What you're looking for is almost a roll of haddock, like rolling meat up for a joint
3. Put the sliced onion on a baking tray and sit the fish on top. Drizzle with oil and put into the oven at 180°C for 12-15 minutes
4. Slice the larger mushrooms, leaving the smaller ones whole. Put a frying pan onto the hob on a moderate heat. Drizzle about 1 tablespoon of oil into the pan and add the mushrooms, adding the larger ones first. The trick is not to add too many to the pan. Turn them over regularly until they are brown
5. When they are brown, add a knob of butter and season with a little pinch of salt and pepper. Also add the sprigs of thyme if using. Cook until the butter has foamed up

To serve:
Serve with whatever vegetables or potatoes you like. Put the fish next to them on a plate, and pour the mushrooms over, along with a little bit of mushroom jus. No, let's call it mushroom juice – we don't want to be too posh about this!

Pollock fillet with wild garlic pesto

They say eat pollock instead of cod, but I think it's now more expensive than cod in a lot of places. That shows we're eating more of it, or what they're catching isn't the quantity we're now demanding. I don't know whether that's right or wrong. But in the meantime I'll tell you how to cook it!
You can use any white fish for this dish – it works well with coley, cod, ling and hake.

Ingredients

4 pollock fillets, 225-250g each
½ white onion, sliced
8 tbsp wild garlic pesto (see page 181 for recipe)
Rapeseed or any other oil, for cooking
Plain flour, to dust the fish
Salt and pepper, to season

Method

1. Lightly flour the fish and season with salt and pepper
2. Put the onions on a baking tray and place the fish on top. Drizzle with oil
3. Put in an oven at 180°C and roast for about 5-6 minutes
4. Take it out, smother with the garlic pesto and put it back in the oven for another 4 minutes. If the fish is thicker than 1 inch, it may need a couple of minutes extra. Use a knife to check if it's cooked – you want it not quite cooked in the middle, as it will carry on cooking with the residual heat. It will be perfectly cooked by the time it gets to the table, not dried out

To serve:
The serving suggestion for this would be good tasty potato wedges with the skins on. You could even have it with chips, or whatever vegetables you'd like really. Pan-fried courgettes would be good, and it'd work well with salad

Chef's tip:

If you've got a little bit left over, don't waste it. Mixed with mayonnaise it would make a fantastic dip or spread. We like second day snack meals!

Red mullet roasted whole with cherry vine tomatoes and basil oil

This is one of my favourites. It's very simple, and eats really well.

Ingredients

8 whole red mullets

16 cherry tomatoes on the vine

½ white onion, sliced

1 lemon

Drizzle basil oil (see page 179 for recipe)

Flour, to dust the fish

Salt and pepper, to season

Basil stalks or leaves (optional)

Method

1. Score the fish and lightly dust with flour. Stuff the cavities with chunks of the lemon, or the basil stalks or leaves if using
2. Put the sliced onion on a baking tray, put the fish on top and season with salt and pepper
3. Snip the vines into groups of 4 tomatoes and place them on the tray next to the fish. Baste everything with the basil oil
4. Roast in the oven for 5 minutes at 200°C

To serve:

I like to serve this with a nice sauté potato. It's great with greens – a fresh kale or something like that. Red mullet is normally in English waters in September and October, when you've got kale and cabbages coming in season, so it works well with them, as well as one of the superfoods, broccoli

Skate wing roasted with chorizo, paprika and spring onions

Skate is actually part of the shark family. Skate has become a generic name for ray wings, but be careful to check with your trusted fishmonger that it's not one of the rays that are protected. To eat, blonde ray are my favourite. It's got a cartilage bone in the middle, so to eat you scrape off one side then turn it over and scrape off the other. You'd be amazed how many people in the restaurant only scrape one side! I like to use the slightly larger skate wings. If they're too big we cut them in half. This is a very popular dish.

Ingredients

4 skate wings, approx 340g each

170g chorizo, chopped

½ white onion, sliced

1 level tsp paprika

Small bunch chopped spring onions

Oil, to cook

4 knobs of butter

Flour, to dust the fish

Salt and pepper, to season

Method

1. Pre-heat the oven to 200°C
2. Lightly flour the skate. Put the sliced white onion on the tray and put the fish on top. Drizzle with oil and season with salt and pepper. Put in the oven for 12 minutes
3. Take it out and top each fish with a sprinkle of paprika, the chopped chorizo and a knob of butter. Return to the oven for a further 6 minutes
4. Take the tray out again and top the fish with the chopped spring onions. Put it back into the oven for a further 1 minute
5. Take out and let it rest for 1 minute before serving

To serve:

It's great on top of roasted vegetables, or with chips. Don't forget to pour the oil from the tray onto the fish

Herrings with rosemary, sea salt and lemon with new potatoes

Herrings were fished out in the 1970s and the authorities of the day closed the fishery. This led to the disappearance of herrings from the local fishmonger and the fish-eating public gradually forgot how to cook them. A Crab House favourite is just to simply bake or grill them using a heavy grill pan.

Ingredients

12 medium-sized herrings

200g mixed salad leaves

1 lemon (sliced)

100ml salad dressing of your choice

Fresh rosemary

4 tbsp rapeseed oil

1 cup medium-coarse sea salt

Black pepper

Cooked new potatoes

Method

1. Take the herrings, gut and clean and put some rosemary sprigs and a piece of lemon into the belly
2. Using a sharp knife, make 3-4 slash cuts (through to the bone) at an interval of 1 centimetre, starting at the thickest part behind the head
3. Place the herrings onto a baking tray, take the medium-coarse sea salt and sprinkle very liberally over the fish. Place more rosemary and lemon pieces on top and drizzle with the rapeseed oil. Place into a hot oven, 200°C, for 8 minutes
4. Alternatively, pan-grill the herrings by placing them cut side down in an oiled heavy grill pan for 2 minutes. Turn over and cook for a further 3 minutes
5. Meanwhile, dress the mixed salad leaves on a plate or board accompanied by the new potatoes. I like cut potatoes, which tends to stop them rolling about on the plate. Place the fish on top of the potatoes and leaves, sprinkle with more fresh rosemary

Chef's tip:

Herrings are a great fish and hugely nutritious, packed with Omega 3.

Classic mussels

At the Crab House Café we strive to use the best quality ingredients and have always preferred rope-grown mussels.

Ingredients

1kg clean, rope-grown mussels (note: if the mussels are seabed-grown they will have thicker, heavier shells so you may need to up the quantity by 500g)

2 cloves garlic, finely diced

2 medium shallots, finely diced

¼ medium-sized lemon cut into 2 wedges

200ml white wine

350ml double cream

3g fresh thyme, including the stalks

1 good pinch cracked black pepper

Method

1. Start by rinsing your mussels under cold water, checking to make sure they are all closed. Any open mussels need to be discarded as do any that float (if they are very slightly open, give them a tap on the side of the sink; if they close up, they are fine to use)
2. Check all the beards have been removed. If the beards are still attached to side of the mussels, remove them by gently pulling them away. It is very important they are all removed otherwise this can make the dish gritty and unpleasant to eat
3. Place all your clean mussels in a large saucepan making sure there is enough room for them to open; once they do they will take up twice as much space. Now add the white wine, chopped shallots, garlic and pepper and bring to the boil. Take the lemon wedges, squeeze over the mussels and drop them in
4. Place the lid on the saucepan and cook for 3-4 minutes on full heat or until all the mussels have opened – a good hard shake of the pan can encourage this. If using seabed-grown mussels, this may take longer
5. Remove the lid, add the cream and simmer for 2-3 minutes without the lid
6. Take the mussels off the heat and serve. I like to serve this dish rustic style with the thyme saved to garnish the top of the dish

Chef's tip:

Ideal served with rustic chunky chips (see the recipe on page 175).

Whole baked plaice with anchovy butter

If possible, make sure the plaice is bought between April and December otherwise the fish is likely to be thin-fleshed as it will be in poor condition after spawning. Serve this dish with vegetables of your choice; I like the smaller plaice as a light supper with brown bread to mop up the juices.

Ingredients

*8 small plaice – 150-200g each
or 4 portions – 400-500g each*
*200g anchovy butter (see page
174 for recipe)*
½ white onion, sliced
2 lemons
Flour, for dusting
Parsley, chopped
Drizzle vegetable oil
Black pepper

Method

1. Take a whole portion-sized plaice or 2 small ones per person. Fish bought from a fishmonger will be gutted, if not, you will need to gut. The smaller ones tend to be fatter and have more flesh-to-bone ratio. You can leave the head on or off at this stage
2. Criss-cross the dark side of the fish and dust with the flour, making sure both sides are coated
3. Spread the onions on a baking tray to act as a trivet and stop the fish sticking and to allow heat under the fish so it cooks evenly. Place the fish on top and spread with the anchovy butter. Sprinkle with black pepper and drizzle with vegetable oil to stop the butter from burning and then roast in an oven at 200°C for 10 minutes, 8 minutes for a small fish
4. Take out of the oven, rest under foil for 1 minute and serve

Alternative method:

1. If you don't want the oil and the mess of cleaning a roasting tray you can use a sheet of tin foil placed on a large baking tray
2. In this case, place the coated fish and onions in the centre of the foil. Fold up the edges over the fish to make a parcel and bake for 10-12 minutes. This method will give great results – if you open this at the table the smell will create a real 'wow factor'
3. Steaming the fish with anchovy butter rather than roasting it will give a more moist texture to the fish. It is harder to overcook it this way too

Desserts

Bourbon whisky chocolate tart with whisky cream

Ingredients

For the tart:

250g bourbon biscuits

500ml double cream

250g dark chocolate buttons

125g unsalted butter

50-75ml bourbon whisky, to

taste

Method

1. Melt butter in the microwave for 30 seconds or until completely melted
2. Whilst your butter is melting, bash bourbon biscuits to an even crumb. I use the end of a rolling pin. Add the butter to the biscuit so it holds together, press firmly into a 8-10 inch tart case, and pop in fridge for 1 hour
3. Whilst the case is setting, put your chocolate buttons in a pan and cover them with cream. It will use about 500ml. Heat gently, stirring with a wooden spoon. Once it is all incorporated, add the bourbon whisky. Taste it and adjust to your preference
4. Leave to cool slightly, then add chocolate to the tart case. Put back in the fridge for 1-2 hours until ready to serve

For the cream:

250ml cream

100ml bourbon whisky

2 tbsp icing sugar

1. Whip the cream and icing sugar until it holds its shape, fold in the whisky
2. You should have a hint of whisky and a semi-sweet cream. This is a very rich dessert; you will not need a lot

Adam's cucumber panna cotta with strawberry soup

This is a recipe Adam came up with after a discussion between us. It reminds me of a strawberry and cucumber Pimms drink. It's been well received by customers and in the restaurant trade. In fact, we've even heard of a Michelin star restaurant in Perth, Australia having a go at it!

Ingredients

1 large cucumber

250g milk

250g cream

150g caster sugar

1 vanilla pod

3 sheets leaf gelatine

Strawberry syrup:

250g or 1 punnet strawberries

150g sugar

4 tbsp water

Splash of balsamic vinegar (optional)

Method

1. Soak your gelatine in cold water for 5 minutes until soft, then juice your cucumber or chop up and add to a pan with milk, cream, vanilla pod and sugar
2. Once this comes up to a simmer, squeeze out the excess water from the gelatine, and whisk into your milk and cream; take off heat, then blitz in a food processor or hand blender and pour through a sieve into a jug
3. Fill up your panna cotta moulds tight to the top and pop in the fridge for 1 hour
4. Whilst your panna cottas are chilling, put your strawberries in a pan with the sugar and water (you could use a touch of red wine or blackcurrant juice, but water should be enough) and bring to a simmer for 5 minutes until the strawberries have cooked out. You could also add a splash of balsamic vinegar at this stage to bring out the fruitiness
5. Blitz to a smooth soup consistency. If it's thick just add more water, then pop in the fridge to cool
6. To serve, add your panna cotta to a hot cup of water for 10 seconds to release the edges, put your strawberry 'soup' around the outside and garnish with fresh mint and summer fruits

Rhubarb fool with orange shortbreads

Ingredients

For the shortbread:

100g butter (softened)

150g plain flour

100g caster sugar

Zest of half an orange

For the fool:

300g rhubarb, cut into 2cm
pieces

500ml double cream

250g mascarpone cheese

200g caster sugar

150g icing sugar

Splash rhubarb liqueur
(optional)

1 vanilla pod (split length ways
and scraped out)

1 star anise

1 cinnamon stick

Method

1. Pre-heat your oven to 180°C. Sieve flour into a bowl, and rub your butter into the flour with your fingers until you have fine breadcrumbs
2. Add your zest and sugar and bring together to form a dough. Transfer to a dusted work surface, roll out to 5 millimetres thickness and bake on greaseproof paper for 8-10 minutes or until a light golden brown
3. Leave on wire rack to cool

1. Add your rhubarb, caster sugar, star anise and cinnamon to a pan and cook for 5 minutes or until rhubarb is tender (you shouldn't need to add water as the rhubarb has so much in it). Allow to cool
2. Meanwhile, whip your cream then add your icing sugar, mascarpone, vanilla and liqueur (if using), until well combined
3. When the rhubarb mix is cool, fold into the cream. Chill. We like to add a few extra pieces of rhubarb on top
4. Serve with your orange shortbread – mine is not in the picture as someone foolishly ate it, so I've had an espresso instead!

Poached pears with lavender and honey

We do this dish in late summer often when we have abundant lavender in the garden.

Ingredients

6 good-sized pears

400ml white wine

100ml honey

6-12 lavender flowers or

1 heaped tbsp of dried lavender

and vanilla pod

Method

1. Place honey and lavender into a small tall-sided saucepan and heat to infuse together
2. Peel and core the pears leaving them whole. Place into the syrup in the pan, it's good to keep them all squashed up, some upside down to fit in tightly and be covered in syrup
3. Poach on a low heat for 20 minutes or until pears are soft
4. Tip into bowl, cover with clingfilm and cool. Leave to marinate overnight if possible. These will keep in fridge for up to 4 days
5. I like to serve in a bowl, one pear stood up and a pear cut in half in a dessert bowl. Pour over some poaching liquor and garnish with lavender flowers. Can be served with ice cream or chocolate sauce or both!

Beetroot cheesecake with compressed oranges

Ingredients

2 large red beetroots

250g full fat cream cheese

1 pack digestive or bourbon biscuits

150g icing sugar or one small pack

150g double cream

125g unsalted butter

200g caster sugar (optional)

100ml water (optional)

Method

1. First boil your beetroot until soft – it will take at least 1 hour. Peel off the skin and blitz with the icing sugar. When this has cooled completely add it to your full fat cream cheese, mix well until incorporated, taste for sweetness and adjust if you require it sweeter

2. Break up your digestives or bourbon biscuits to an even crumb and add melted butter. Mix well then press into a tart case, or single moulds. You want about 1.5 centimetre base. Put in the fridge for half an hour

3. Add your mix and smooth off with palate knife. Put in the fridge for 1 hour

4. Cut the skin off the orange with a sharp knife. We compress our oranges for sweetness, but if you boil 200g caster sugar with 100 millilitre water until it starts to bubble, you can then pour that over your oranges, leave to cool, and it will have a similar effect

Chef's tip:

This cheesecake also works well with chocolate sauce – just melt chocolate, butter and double cream together.

Cinnamon doughnuts with apple compote

Ingredients

For the doughnuts:

1½kg plain flour

700ml milk

½ tbsp dried active baking yeast

205g caster sugar

175g butter

5 egg yolks

1½ litres oil

2 tbsp warm water

Method

1. Add water and 1 teaspoon of the sugar to the yeast in a small bowl and mix until pasty. Set aside and let it rise until spongy
2. Scald milk with butter and cool to a lukewarm temperature
3. Beat the egg yolks. Add the sugar and mix thoroughly. Add the cooled scalded milk mixture and beat until foamy. Mix in the yeast mixture. Add the flour gradually, beating after addition to make a soft dough. Beat until thick and springy, but not too much because it will make the doughnuts hard. Cover, and let it rise until doubled in size
4. Shape dough into small balls. Let them rise on floured greaseproof paper until they've doubled
5. In a deep fat fryer, heat the oil to 190°C. Fry the doughnuts until brown, then roll in sugar and cool

For the apple compote:

3 dessert apples, peeled and cored

50g butter

1 vanilla pod, split lengthways and scraped out

½ tsp cinnamon

1 tbsp caster sugar

1 tbsp water

1. Cut the apples into half-centimetre cubes then add to a saucepan with the rest of the ingredients. Slowly cook until tender

Crab House summer pudding

Ingredients

2 x 340g packs frozen fruits

2 loaves sliced white bread

125g icing sugar

Method

1. Empty the frozen fruit into a bowl and either leave on the side for 2 hours or in the fridge overnight. I pour my sugar over the fruit while they are defrosting

2. When the fruits have defrosted, mix gently to incorporate the sugar then strain the juice gently from the berries without crushing your fruits. You can add a little water at the start to stretch the juice a little. Taste – it needs to be tart

3. Cut out your circles of bread; you want 3 circles to a portion. Dip your circles into the juice on both sides, so your bread has absorbed all the flavour and covered

4. Press into your mould, then add a tablespoon of fruit, then a layer of bread, then a layer of fruit, then 1 more layer or bread. Press down well and chill for half an hour

5. Serve with clotted cream, ice cream and a few fresh berries to garnish. Don't be afraid to adjust recipes and always taste as you go – this is the secret to most cooking

Chef's tip:

Alternatively, you could use an equivalent weight of fresh, seasonal soft fruit.

Elderflower jellies with Alexander sugar

I am a great believer of using ingredients together that grow together in their natural habitat; they seem to always work in harmony with one another. The most common example of this is apple and blackberry, both found in hedges in late summer or in your orchard. And there is nothing more satisfying than to have it free from the hedgerows. Hence this recipe idea of mine. We are able to do this at the end of May time when the elderflowers are out. Elderflowers make wonderful syrups that can then be used for desserts, drinks and in this case, a jelly. Alexanders grow everywhere on the side of coastal roads. They were brought to England by the Romans and they ate the leaves, stems, root and buds. It's a bit like a very aromatic celery or parsley, sometimes called horse parsley, due to horses having it as feed. It is a great one to forage; some books have recipes to turn the stem into angelica, like stems for dessert garnish. This gave me the idea of making a green sugar with Alexanders.

Ingredients

To make the Alexander sugar:
100g Alexander leaves
250g granulated sugar

To make the elderflower syrup:
500g elderflowers
2 lemons, zest and juice
2kg sugar
2 litres water

To make the jelly:
200g mixed summer fruits
(strawberries, raspberries etc) or
poached pear, diced
250ml elderflower syrup
250ml Champagne or sparkling
wine
5 sheets gelatine leaves

Method

1. Blanch the Alexander leaves in boiling water to fix the colour and to sterilise
2. Pat dry, put into a blender with the sugar and blitz until sugar is green and of caster sugar consistency. This will keep in an airtight container for several months, but the light will start to fade the colour

1. Put sugar, lemon juice and the zest into a saucepan with the water and bring to the boil, then pour over the elderflowers and leave to steep for 4 days in a cool place
2. Strain and bottle. It will keep for 6 weeks if kept cool.
3. Use for desserts etc and jelly

1. Soak the gelatine sheets in cold water until soft
2. Bring the elderflower syrup to boil, set aside and squeeze water from the gelatine that has soaked and stir into hot syrup until dissolved
3. Cool down until nearly setting; gently stir in sparkling wine or Champagne and fruit; pour into chilled jelly moulds

To serve:
Turn the jelly out onto a plate, garnish with the Alexander sugar and serve with vanilla ice cream

Drop scones with blueberry and apple

Ingredients

125g self raising flour

2 tsp caster sugar

1 egg, beaten

150ml buttermilk

4 tsp vegetable/sunflower oil

1 tbsp melted butter

For the filling:

150g blueberries

200g apple, peeled and cut into small chunks

100g caster sugar

25g butter

Method

1. Put your flour in a bowl with the sugar and make a well. Add your egg and melted butter and gradually the milk, mix as you are doing this until you have a nice thick batter

2. Grease your pan with oil and put it on a medium heat. Add a tablespoon worth of batter. It will form in the pan as a circle and bubble up. Cook for about 90 seconds on each side until golden brown

3. For the filling, add half the sugar, water and blueberries to a pan and cook out on a medium heat for 10 minutes or until syrupy. Allow to cool

4. Cook the apple in a non-stick pan with the rest of the sugar. Add the butter until it melts and coats the apple. Then take off the heat and allow to cool

To serve:

It's a great idea to keep the pancakes warm so they keep their fluffy texture. Layer the pancakes with the fruit – first blueberry, then apple, and so on. Served with clotted cream, ice cream or even yoghurt

Chef's tip:

Any poached fruit is really good with pancakes. You could mix the apples and blueberries together.

Basic Recipes

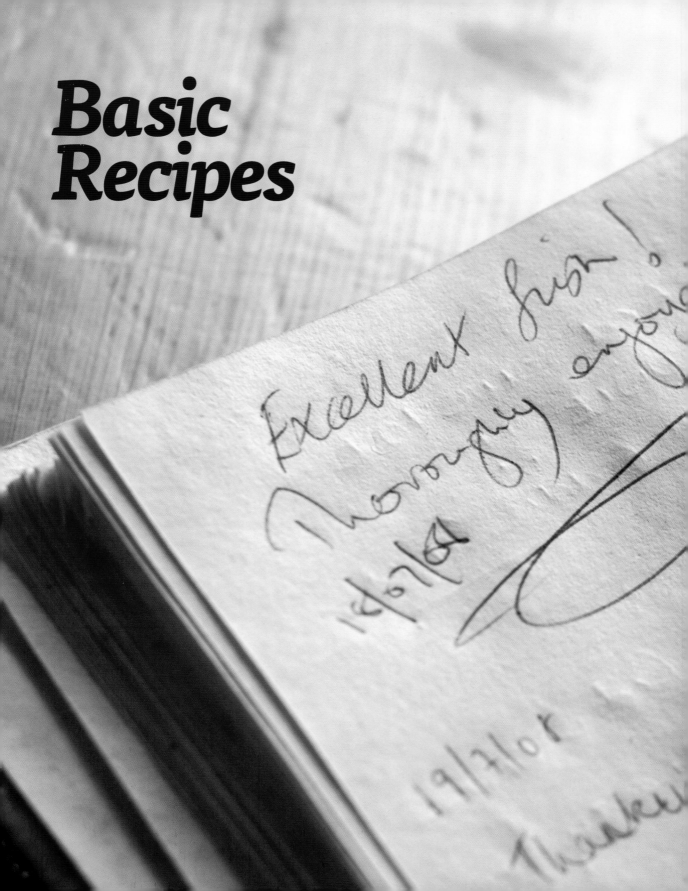

Base curry sauce

Here's how to make a curry base called marsalla gravy. It will make enough for approximately 10 curries. If you don't have the room for any excess, just make the ingredients smaller as required – the rest is the same. But if you can, do make more to freeze as it freezes really well.

Ingredients

300ml ghee or vegetable oil

500g garlic and ginger mix (see page 181 for recipe)

10 large Spanish onions, approx 3-3.5kg

6 tbsp tomato purée

1 tsp salt

2 tbsp turmeric

4 tbsp curry powder

1-6 tbsp chilli powder (to taste)

2 tbsp ground cumin seeds

2 tbsp fresh coriander leaves, finely chopped

Method

1. Coarsely chop the onions, then boil them for 5 minutes – use the same weight of water as there is of onions. Drain, then blend to a fine texture
2. Mix the turmeric, curry powder, chilli powder, cumin seeds and coriander leaves with water to make a paste, of the consistency of tomato sauce
3. Heat the oil and stir-fry the garlic and ginger mix for about 6 minutes. Add the spice paste and stir-fry until the water has evaporated and the oil separates – approximately 5 minutes. If it needs it, add water to make the gravy pourable
4. Add the onion purée and stir-fry for 10 minutes. Add the tomato purée and stir-fry for another 10 minutes, then add the salt
5. Portion into 10 and freeze any you don't immediately require

Tartare sauce

Some like tartare sauce to be quite smooth. We tend to like it chunky.

Ingredients

250g homemade or good quality shop bought mayonnaise

100g gherkins or pickled cucumbers

50g capers

Zest and juice of 1 lemon

Pinch of ground black pepper

Method

1. Combine all ingredients and pulse to your preferred consistency

Basic tomato sauce

Ingredients

1kg chopped tomatoes

500g chopped or sliced white onion

5 cloves crushed garlic

1 tsp of salt

500ml water

2 tbsp fresh or dried oregano, or any other herbs of your liking

1 tbsp rapeseed or any other oil

Method

1. Heat the oil in a large pan over a low-medium heat. Add the onion and sweat until soft and translucent. The best way to do this is with the lid on, which will create steam. You're not looking to colour the onion, so add a little water if it starts to catch
2. Add the garlic and oregano or herbs and sweat for a further minute
3. Add the tomatoes, along with the salt and water
4. Simmer until reduced by half, giving it a good stir occasionally to make sure it doesn't catch on the bottom. Taste and adjust the seasoning if necessary

Chef's tip:

If you want a stronger tomato taste, add a little balsamic vinegar. It brings out the sharpness of the fruit and makes tinned tomatoes taste like fresh ones! This is a great sauce to keep. It will keep in the fridge for 4 or 5 days, and it freezes and defrosts very well too. It's great to spread on your own pizzas as a base or to stir into pasta – add some chilli for an arrabiata. Blitz it with a little bit of cream to make a cream of tomato soup. Or you could add lots of vinegar and call it ketchup!

Fish stock

Ingredients

1kg fish bones, and heads [optional – ask your fishmonger to remove the gills or they will turn your stock grey and cloudy]

4 litres water

Method

1. Add the fish bones and water to a large pan. Bring it to a simmer – not a boil – and cook for 20 minutes
2. Let it cool, put a colander or sieve into the pan and ladle out the clear stock
3. If you simmer the stock for longer than 20 minutes, you will be left with a thick white stock, which can sometimes be better for use in stews

Chef's tip:

Freeze the fish stock into ice cubes for use at a later date

Mixed herb butter

Ingredients

250g salted butter
40g of mixed herbs of your
preference. I used 10g chives,
10g parsley, 10g tarragon, 10g
thyme (including the stock). This
could also be done with
individual herbs e.g., tarragon
butter, parsley butter etc.

Method

1. First, cut the block of butter in half lengthways and then both halves into 6 widthways, leaving you with 12 small blocks
2. Place in a bowl and microwave on full power for 30 seconds. Alternatively you could leave the block of butter out on the window sill for an hour or two. We need a soft, pliable consistency, not melted
3. Chop the mixed herbs finely. If you are using thyme like me, strip and discard the stalks
4. Add to the butter and beat together with a wooden spoon until you are happy that the herbs are evenly spread throughout
5. Take clingfilm and lay it flat on your work surface. Place the butter in a pile about two-thirds of the way in from the end
6. Fold the short end of the clingfilm over the butter and roll into a sausage shape. Twist and tie the ends then place in the fridge for 2-3 hours
7. Once firm, the herb butter can be easily cut into the quantity you require and the rest saved for another day

Anchovy butter

A great store cupboard butter which will keep in the fridge and can be frozen.

Ingredients

340g tin anchovies
500g butter

Method

1. Tip the anchovies into a blender, along with the oil from the tin
2. Add the butter and blend together until emulsified

Rustic chunky chips

Ingredients

4-6 large potatoes. I would use either Maris Pipers or King Edwards but Cara, Romaro and Pentland Crown are also very good

Method

1. Start by peeling your potatoes
2. Cut into evenly shaped chips around 1.5 centimetres thick and 5 centimetres long
3. Give the chips a quick rinse/wash, place into a colander and allow to dry for a minute or 2, but not so long they go brown
4. Place into the deep fat fryer at 130°C for 5-6 minutes or until they just start to become soft not crisp. Take them out and place in a bowl with a tea towel or kitchen paper at the bottom and allow the excess fat to drain off. We would now say the chips are par-cooked or blanched
5. Next, turn up the fryer to 190°C and wait until you are five minutes before serving. At this time, put the chips back in the fryer for a further 4-5 minutes or until nicely crisp. Enjoy

Chef's tip:

Why not try one of the great mayonnaises from this section of the book to accompany the chips?

Light beer batter

Ingredients

110g self-raising flour
150ml sparkling water or beer
Salt and pepper, to season

Method

1. Sift the flour into a mixing bowl and season
2. Gradually add the water or beer, whisking continuously until the batter is smooth and at your desired consistency. If it's too thick, add a bit more water or beer

Chef's tip:

It's important to let the batter stand for a while before using it. You can flavour your batter however you want. If you want a spicy batter, put a bit of cayenne in. Lemon, horseradish... anything you like. If you're using beer, it has to be fizzy – a real ale straight out of the keg isn't going to have the same effect. You could use a bottle of conditioned beer – how about Crab House Mussel Ale or Oyster Stout?

Aioli

Ingredients

300ml homemade or good quality
shop bought mayonnaise

3 cloves crushed garlic

12 strands saffron

2 tbsp hot water

Juice 1 lemon

Salt and pepper, to season

Method

1. Put the saffron strands in a teacup and pour the hot water over. Add the lemon juice and let the saffron steep – that is, let it release its colour, alost like brewing tea
2. Put the saffron-infused water, mayonnaise and garlic in a blender and blitz to a smooth consistency
3. Taste and adjust the seasoning to your liking

Béchamel sauce

Ingredients

500ml milk

½ white onion

1 bay leaf

2 cloves

50g butter

50g plain flour

Salt and pepper, to season

Method

1. Gently bring the milk to the boil in a small saucepan. Add the onion, bay leaf and cloves, turn off the heat and leave to infuse for 20 minutes
2. In another saucepan, melt the butter, then add the flour. Stir continuously until they form a paste or 'roux'. Continue cooking for 2 minutes
3. Remove the onion, bay leaf and cloves from the milk with a slotted spoon and discard. Add the infused milk to the roux gradually, stirring as you go, until you get a smooth sauce
4. Cook for 5-10 minutes, stirring continuously, until the sauce has thickened to your required consistency. Season to taste

Chef's tip:

Béchamel sauce keeps quite well in a fridge. It's great to make a Welsh rarebit from the next day. We often top fish with rarebit, and sometimes sliced tomatoes too.

Mayonnaise

This is a quick and easy method for mayonnaise and can also be used as a base for sauces such as tartare sauce.

Ingredients

2 large egg yolks

1,200ml sunflower oil

Juice of ½ lemon

50ml white wine vinegar

1 tsp ground white pepper

1 tbsp salt

10ml water

Method

1. Using either a mechanical whisk, food processor or hand whisk, bind together the egg yolks, lemon juice, vinegar, white pepper, salt and water until light and creamy
2. Slowly add the sunflower oil whilst continually whisking. Be careful not to add too much oil at a time to prevent it splitting. Whisk until thick

Hollandaise

You can do all sorts of great variations on hollandaise. Try using lime juice or grapefruit juice instead of lemon juice. Orange juice can also be used, but reduce by half to concentrate otherwise the flavour will be lost. You could add whipped cream to lighten the texture. Chopped gherkins or capers are good, as is tarragon, and you could use tarragon vinegar instead of the cider vinegar for extra flavour. For an added texture, you could also add chopped shallots, along with fennel herb and a little Pernod.

Ingredients

2 tbsp cider vinegar or white wine vinegar

Pinch white pepper

4 egg yolks

250g butter clarified (see how to clarify butter on page 55)

Juice of 1 lemon

Method

1. Heat the vinegar and pepper in a pan and reduce by one third
2. Take off the heat and allow to cool for 2 minutes then whisk in the egg yolks. Return to a gentle heat, whisking continually until the mixture goes frothy and thickens to the 'ribbon stage', which is where you can draw a line on the mixture with the mixture itself and it stays proud for 10 seconds or more. As a young chef, I would try to write my name!
3. Take the sauce off the heat so as not to raise the temperature over 65°C. Slowly add the clarified butter, whisking all the time until it's taken all the butter. It will now be quite thick
4. Season with lemon juice to taste. Keep warm to serve but not hot

Chef's tip:

You can make the hollandaise using a food processor. Add a little cold water to rescue it if it starts to curdle or split, and a little hot water if the sauce is too thick. Remember to check the seasoning to taste.

Orange & nut dressing

Ingredients

100ml French dressing [see below for recipe]

1 orange

2 tbsp toasted walnuts, hazelnuts or cobnuts

Method

1. Into the French dressing, add the zest and juice of the orange
2. Add the nuts
3. Stir

French dressing

This will store in a cool place for two weeks. It will separate but easily comes together again with a good shake. If kept too cold, the oil may cloud or become solid and gloopy – if so just warm and it will clear. The easiest way is to stand it in warm water for a few minutes.

Ingredients

1 tsp Dijon mustard

½ tsp icing sugar

100ml cider vinegar or white wine vinegar

400ml good quality rapeseed or olive oil

¼ teaspoon salt

Method

1. Mix together the mustard, icing sugar, vinegar and salt. Whisk in the oil, a little at first to blend, slowly increasing the flow of whisking all the time until an emulsion is made. Alternately put all ingredients in a food processor and blitz
2. Taste and adjust seasoning to your liking

Chef's tips:

Use lemon juice instead of vinegar – this is particularly good with salads accompanying fish. Try warming the dressing and serving with a warm salad or even on some fish.

Add chopped onions, peppers, chillies and chopped hard fruits – or firmer soft fruit like grapes and melon – for a salsa-style garnish.

Basil oil

Ingredients

100g basil – small leaf green basil (minuet) is very pungent
400ml oil – light olive oil was my favourite but now we've got some English cold-pressed rapeseed oils which are nutty and very good. Fussells is my favourite from up the road in Somerset

Method

1. Quickly blanch the basil in boiling water
2. Dry it off and put in a mixer
3. Pour in the oil and blitz
4. This can be kept in the fridge. Don't worry if it goes cloudy when cold – if you take it out into a warm kitchen for an hour it will go clear again

Roast garlic oil

Ingredients

1 good-sized bulb of garlic or 6 leftover garlic ends
1 litre of light olive oil or rapeseed oil

Method

1. Roast the garlic on a baking tray in a hot oven of around 220°C for about 15 minutes
2. Drop the roasted garlic ends in the olive oil and allow them to infuse for at least 2 days

Preserving lemons

Preserved lemons give a wonderful Middle Eastern fragrance to a dish. It doesn't make the lemons overly salty, but you may not need to season the dish you're adding them to, or at least use less salt.

Ingredients

10-15 unwaxed lemons

400g flaky sea salt {depending on the size of the lemons}

Method

1. Pre-heat oven to a low heat. Take two sealable Kilner-style jars, about 500g capacity in size, and wash them them well in warm soapy water. Rinse thoroughly, and leave them to dry upside down in the oven
2. Scrub the lemons clean and cut them into eighths
3. Once the jars are dry, pack the lemons into them tightly, surrounded by salt. Continue to fill the jars up with layers of lemon and salt. Once you've reached the top, press the lemons down well and finish the jars with a final layer of salt
4. Leave the jars in a cool dark place for at least 3 months before using. Check them every day – there should always be a layer of salt at the bottom of the jars, so add more if needed

Chef's tip:

I sometimes add rosemary or mint to the jars to give the preserved lemons an extra flavour. You could do this with almost any herbs or spices – just pack them in around the lemons along with the salt.

Garlic, ginger & chilli mix (Chinese style)

Ingredients

2 bulbs garlic

*Root ginger, about the size of
your thumb*

1 tbsp fish or soy sauce

2 stalks lemongrass

Method

1. Chop the bottom roots off the garlic and pull the wood from the centre of the bulb. Put into a food processor
2. Peel the ginger. Don't worry about getting every last bit of skin off. Chop roughly and put into the food processor
3. Pour in the fish or soy sauce
4. Chop the lemongrass into small bits and add to the food processor
5. Blitz until it reaches a stuffing-like consistency. This mixture sometimes goes quite green. Don't worry! This is perfectly normal and the colour will disappear in the cooking

Wild garlic pesto

Wild garlic is sometimes known as broad leaf garlic or ramsons. You find it from March 'til the end of May in shaded areas. When it's up it's prolific, so it won't take you long to gather. The flowers are good to eat, as are the bulbs, leaves and stalks. I love garlic, if you hadn't noticed! This is a basic pesto recipe. We're putting wild garlic with it but to be honest you could use rosemary or basil. We don't make it the traditional way with pine nuts. They've gone really expensive at the moment. I've heard of cashews and peanuts being used to make pesto. We're just using mixed nuts.

Ingredients

450g wild garlic leaves

*1 wild garlic bulb, peeled and
chopped*

110g Parmesan cheese

225g mixed nuts

1 litre olive or rapeseed oil

Salt, to season

Method

1. Plunge the garlic leaves into a bowl of boiling water to sterilise them, then straight into a bowl of cold water. Take them out, squeeze out any excess water and chop roughly with a knife. Put the leaves into a mixer
2. Put the mixed nuts and chopped garlic bulb onto a baking tray. Toast in the oven for a few minutes at 180°C until golden brown. Be careful not to burn them – they won't take long
3. Once the nuts are golden brown, take the tray out of the oven and tip into the mixer. Add the Parmesan cheese, oil and a good pinch of salt, and blitz to your liking

Index

Index continued...

Written by:
Nigel Bloxham

Contributors:
Mark Hix, Charlie Bloxham

Edited by:
John Murphy, Adam Kay, Christopher Brierley

Design by:
Richard Abbey

Photography by:
© Tim Green www.timgreenphotographer.co.uk
Additional photographs by Lara Jane Thorpe (www.larajanethorpephotography.com),
Daniel Rushall (www.danielrushall.com) and Crab House Café

First published in 2014 on behalf of:
Crab House Café – www.crabhousecafe.co.uk
Ferryman's Way, Portland Road, Wyke Regis, Dorset DT4 9YU
Tel: 01305 788867

Published by:
RMC Books – www.rmcbooks.co.uk
Broadfield Court, Broadfield Business Park, Sheffield S8 0XF
Tel: 0114 250 6300